CAST *of* CHARACTERS

LOST & FOUND

ENCOUNTERS *with* THE LIVING GOD

MAX LUCADO

THOMAS NELSON
Since 1798

NASHVILLE DALLAS MEXICO CITY RIO DE JANEIRO

Published in Nashville, Tennessee, by Thomas Nelson. Thomas Nelson is a registered trademark of Thomas Nelson, Inc.

Thomas Nelson, Inc., titles may be purchased in bulk for educational, business, fund-raising, or sales promotional use. For information, please e-mail SpecialMarkets@ThomasNelson.com.

ISBN: 978-0-8499-4673-8 (IE)

Library of Congress Control Number: 2012930146

ISBN: 978-0-8499-4737-7

Printed in the United States of America

12 13 14 15 16 QG 6 5 4 3 2 1

I would like to dedicate this book to one of my dearest friends and favorite characters: Art Hill. Longtime elder of the church, husband of my editorial assistant, and all-'round great guy. Thanks for being Art.

ALSO BY MAX LUCADO

CONTENTS

CONTENTS

Chapter 1

❧

JAIRUS

When Jesus went in the boat back to the other side of the lake, a large crowd gathered around him there. A leader of the synagogue, named Jairus, came there, saw Jesus, and fell at his feet. He begged Jesus, saying again and again, "My daughter is dying. Please come and put your hands on her so she will be healed and will live." So Jesus went with him. . . .

While Jesus was still speaking, some people came from the house of the synagogue leader. They said, "Your daughter is dead. There is no need to bother the teacher anymore."

But Jesus paid no attention to what they said. He told the synagogue leader, "Don't be afraid; just believe."

Jesus let only Peter, James, and John the brother of James go with him. When they came to the house of the synagogue leader, Jesus found many people there making lots of noise and crying loudly. Jesus entered the house and said to them, "Why are you crying and making so much noise? The child is not dead, only asleep." But they laughed at him. So, after throwing them out of the house, Jesus took the child's father and mother and his three followers into the room where the child was. Taking hold of the girl's hand, he said to her, "Talitha, koum!" (This means, "Young girl, I tell you to stand up!") At once the girl stood right up and began walking. (She was twelve years old.) Everyone was completely amazed. Jesus gave them strict orders not to tell people about this. Then he told them to give the girl something to eat.

—MARK 5:21–24, 35–43

SEEING THE UNSEEN

When my daughters were young, we tried an experiment.

I asked Jenna, then eight years old, to go to one side of the den. I had Andrea, six, stand on the other. Three-year-old Sara and I sat on the couch in the middle and watched. Jenna's job was to close her eyes and walk. Andrea's job was to be Jenna's eyes and talk her safely across the room.

With phrases like, "Take two baby steps to the left" and, "Take four giant steps straight ahead," Andrea successfully navigated her sister through a treacherous maze of chairs, a vacuum cleaner, and a laundry basket.

Then Jenna took her turn. She guided Andrea past her mom's favorite lamp and shouted just in time to keep her from colliding into the wall when she thought her right foot was her left foot.

After several treks through the darkness, they stopped and we processed.

"I didn't like it," Jenna complained. "It's scary going where you can't see."

"I was afraid I was going to fall," Andrea agreed. "I kept taking little steps to be safe."

I can relate, can't you? We grown-ups don't like the dark either. But we walk in it. We, like Jenna, often complain about how scary it is to walk where we can't see. And we, like Andrea, often take timid steps so we won't fall.

We've reason to be cautious: We are blind. We can't see the future. We have absolutely no vision beyond the present. I can't tell you with certainty that I will live long enough to finish this paragraph. (Whew, I did!) Nor can you tell me you'll live long enough to read the next one. (Hope you do!)

I'm not talking nearsightedness or obstructed view; I'm talking opaque blindness. I'm not talking about a condition that passes with childhood; I'm describing a condition that passes only with death. We are blind. Blind to the future.

It's one limitation we all share. The wealthy are just as blind as the poor. The educated are just as sightless as the unschooled. And the famous know as little about the future as the unknown.

None of us know how our children will turn out. None of us know the day we will die. No one knows whom he or she will marry or even if marriage lies before him or her. We are universally, absolutely, unalterably blind.

We are all Jenna with her eyes shut, groping through a dark room, listening for a familiar voice—but with one difference. Her surroundings are familiar and friendly. Ours can be hostile and fatal. Her worst fear is a stubbed toe. Our worst fear is more threatening: cancer, divorce, loneliness, death.

And try as we might to walk as straight as we can, chances are a toe is going to get stubbed and we are going to get hurt.

Just ask Jairus. He is a man who has tried to walk as straight as he can. But Jairus was a man whose path has taken a sudden turn into a cave—a dark cave. And he doesn't want to enter it alone.

Jairus is the leader of the synagogue. That may not mean much to you and me, but in the days of Christ the leader of the synagogue was the most important man in the community. The synagogue was the center of religion, education, leadership, and social activity. The leader of the synagogue was the senior religious leader, the highest-ranking professor, the mayor, and the best-known citizen all in one.

Jairus has it all. Job security. A guaranteed welcome at the coffee shop. A pension plan. Golf every Thursday and an annual all-expenses-paid trip to the national convention.

Who could ask for more? Yet Jairus does. He *has* to ask for more. In fact, he would trade the whole package of perks and privileges for just one assurance—that his daughter will live.

The Jairus we see in this story is not the clear-sighted, black-frocked, nicely groomed civic leader. He is instead a blind man begging for a gift. He fell at Jesus' feet, "saying again and again, 'My daughter is dying. Please come and put your hands on her so she will be healed and will live'" (Mark 5:23).

He doesn't barter with Jesus. ("You do me a favor, and I'll see you are taken care of for life.") He doesn't negotiate with Jesus. ("The guys in Jerusalem are getting pretty testy about your antics. Tell you what, you handle this problem of mine, and I'll make a few calls . . .") He doesn't make excuses. ("Normally, I'm not this desperate, Jesus, but I've got a small problem.")

He just pleads.

There are times in life when everything you have to offer is nothing compared to what you are asking to receive. Jairus is at such a point. What could a man offer in exchange for his child's life? So there are no games. No haggling. No masquerades. The situation is starkly simple: Jairus is blind to the future and Jesus knows the future. So Jairus asks for his help.

And Jesus, who loves the honest heart, goes to give it.

And God, who knows what it is like to lose a child, empowers his son.

But before Jesus and Jairus get very far, they are interrupted by emissaries from Jairus's house.

"Your daughter is dead. There is no need to bother the teacher anymore" (v. 35).

Get ready. Hang on to your hat. Here's where the story gets moving. Jesus goes from being led to leading, from being convinced by Jairus to *convincing* Jairus. From being admired to being laughed at, from helping out the people to casting out the people.

Here is where Jesus takes control.

"But Jesus paid no attention to what they said . . ." (v. 36).

I love that line! It describes the critical principle for seeing the unseen: Ignore what people say. Block them out. Turn them off. Close your ears. And, if you have to, walk away.

Ignore the ones who say it's too late to start over.

Disregard those who say you'll never amount to anything.

Turn a deaf ear toward those who say that you aren't smart enough, fast enough, tall enough, or big enough—ignore them.

Faith sometimes begins by stuffing your ears with cotton.

Jesus turns immediately to Jairus and pleads: "Don't be afraid; just believe" (v. 36).

Jesus compels Jairus to see the unseen. When Jesus says, "Just believe . . . ," he is imploring, "Don't limit your possibilities to the visible. Don't listen only for the audible. Don't be controlled by the logical. Believe there is more to life than meets the eye!"

"Trust me," Jesus is pleading. "Don't be afraid; just trust."

A father in the Bahamas cried out the same plea to his young son who was trapped in a burning house. The two-story structure was engulfed in flames, and the family—the father, mother, and several children—was on its way out when the smallest boy became terrified and ran back upstairs. His father, outside, shouted to him: "Jump, son, jump! I'll catch you." The boy cried: "But Daddy, I can't see you." "I know," his father called, "but I can see you."

The father could see, even though the son could not.

A similar example of faith was found on the wall of a concentration camp. On it a prisoner had carved the words:

> *I believe in the sun, even though it doesn't shine,*
> *I believe in love, even when it isn't shown,*
> *I believe in God, even when he doesn't speak.*

I try to imagine the person who etched those words. I try to envision his skeletal hand gripping the broken glass or stone that cut into the wall. I try to imagine his eyes squinting through the darkness as he carved each letter. What hand could have cut such a conviction? What eyes could have seen good in such horror?

There is only one answer: eyes that chose to see the unseen.

As Paul wrote: "We set our eyes not on what we see but on what we cannot see. What we see will last only a short time, but what we cannot see will last forever" (2 Cor. 4:18).

Jesus is asking Jairus to see the unseen. To make a choice. Either to live by the facts or to see by faith. When tragedy strikes we, too, are left to choose what we see. We can see either the hurt or the Healer.

The choice is ours.

Jairus made his choice. He opted for faith and Jesus . . . and faith *in* Jesus led him to his daughter.

At the house Jesus and Jairus encounter a group of mourners. Jesus is troubled by their wailing. It bothers him that they express such anxiety over death. "Why are you crying and making so much noise? The child is not dead, only asleep" (v. 39).

That's not a rhetorical question. It's an honest one. From his perspective, the girl is not dead—she is only asleep. From God's viewpoint, death is not permanent. It is a necessary step for passing from this world to the next. It's not an end; it's a beginning.

As a young boy I had two great loves—playing and eating. Summers were made for afternoons on the baseball diamond and meals at Mom's dinner table. Mom had a rule, however. Dirty, sweaty boys could never eat at the table. Her first words to us as we came home were always, "Go clean up and take off those clothes if you want to eat."

Now, no boy is fond of bathing and dressing, but I never once complained and defied my mom by saying, "I'd rather stink than eat!" In my economy a bath and a clean shirt were a small price to pay for a good meal.

And from God's perspective death is a small price to pay for the privilege of sitting at his table. "Flesh and blood cannot have a part in the kingdom of God. . . . This body that can be destroyed *must* clothe itself with something that can never be destroyed. And this body that dies *must* clothe itself with something that can never die" (1 Cor. 15:50, 53; emphasis added).

God is even more insistent than my mom was. In order to sit at his table, a change of clothing *must* occur. And we must die in order for our body to be exchanged for a new one. So, from God's viewpoint, death is not to be dreaded; it is to be welcomed.

And when he sees people crying and mourning over death, he wants to know, "Why are you crying?" (v. 39).

When we see death, we see disaster. When Jesus sees death, he sees deliverance.

That's too much for the people to take. "They laughed at him" (v. 40). (The next time people mock you, you might remember they mocked him too.)

Now look closely because you aren't going to believe what Jesus does next. He throws the mourners out! That's what the text says, "after throwing them out of the house . . ." (v. 40). He doesn't just ask them to leave. He *throws* them out. He picks them up by collar and belt and sets them sailing. Jesus' response was decisive and strong. In the original text, the word used here is the same word used to describe what Jesus did to the money changers in the temple. It's the same verb used *thirty-eight* times to describe what Jesus did to the demons.

Why? Why such force? Why such intolerance?

Perhaps the answer is found by going back to my family's living room experience. After Jenna and Andrea had taken turns guiding each other through the den, I decided to add a diabolical twist. On the last trip, I snuck up behind Jenna, who was walking with her eyes shut, and began whispering, "Don't listen to her. Listen to me. I'll take care of you."

Jenna stopped. She analyzed the situation and made her choice between the two voices. "Be quiet, Daddy," she giggled and then continued in Andrea's direction.

Undeterred, I grabbed the lid of a pan, held it next to her ear, and banged it with a spoon. She jumped and stopped, startled by the noise. Andrea, seeing that her pilgrim was frightened, did a great thing. She ran across the room and threw her arms around her sister and said, "Don't worry, I'm right here."

She wasn't about to let the noise distract Jenna from the journey.

And God isn't going to let the noise distract you from yours. He's still busy casting out the critics and silencing the voices that could deter you.

Some of his work you have seen. Most of it you haven't.

Only when you get home will you know how many times he has protected you from luring voices. Only eternity will reveal the time he:

> Interfered with the transfer, protecting you from involvement in unethical business.
>
> Fogged in the airport, distancing you from a shady opportunity.
>
> Flattened your tire, preventing you from checking into the hotel and meeting a seductive man.

And only heaven will show the times he protected you by:

> Giving you a mate who loves God more than you do.
>
> Opening the door for a new business so you could attend the same church.
>
> Having the right voice with the right message on the right radio station the day you needed his encouragement.

Mark it down: God knows you and I are blind. He knows living by faith and not by sight doesn't come naturally. And I think that's one reason he raised Jairus's daughter from the dead. Not for her sake—she was better off in heaven. But for our sake—to teach us that heaven sees when we trust.

One final thought from the seeing-with-your-eyes-closed experiment. I asked Jenna how she could hear Andrea's voice guiding her across the room when I was trying to distract her by whispering in her ear.

Her answer? "I just concentrated and listened as hard as I could."

QUESTIONS FOR REFLECTION AND DISCUSSION

1. What did you think of Max's "faith experiment" with his daughters? What was he trying to teach them? What did you learn from his experiment?

2. Do you ever wish you could see into the future? What would be the benefits of doing so? The drawbacks? If you could acquire the ability to see your whole future, would you do so? Explain.

3. Max claims that a critical principle for seeing the unseen is to ignore what people say. What does he mean? What sort of people do you ignore? What kinds of advice do you refuse to heed? Couldn't Max's advice be dangerous in some circumstances? In what kind of circumstances?

4. Why did Jesus throw the people out of Jairus's home?

5. Read 2 Corinthians 4:16–18. How permanent is the world we see? How permanent is the world we do not see? How do we "set our eyes" on Jesus?

Chapter 2

❧

SIMON AND MARY

Mary brought in a pint of very expensive perfume made from pure nard. She poured the perfume on Jesus' feet, and then she wiped his feet with her hair. And the sweet smell from the perfume filled the whole house.

—JOHN 12:3

RISKY LOVE

Artful Eddie lacked nothing. He was the slickest of the slick law-yers. He was one of the roars of the Roaring Twenties. A crony of Al Capone, he ran the gangster's dog tracks. He mastered the simple technique of fixing the race by overfeeding seven dogs and betting on the eighth.

Wealth. Status. Style. Artful Eddie lacked nothing.

Then why did he turn himself in? Why did he offer to squeal on Capone? What was his motive? Didn't Eddie know the surefire conse-quences of ratting on the mob?

He knew, but he'd made up his mind.

What did he have to gain? What could society give him that he didn't have? He had money, power, prestige. What was the hitch?

Eddie revealed the hitch. His son. Eddie had spent his life with the despicable. He had smelled the stench of the underground long enough. For his son, he wanted more. He wanted to give his son a name. And to give his son a name, he would have to clear his own. Eddie was willing to take a risk so that his son could have a clean slate. Artful Eddie never saw his dream come true. After Eddie squealed, the mob remembered. Two shotgun blasts silenced him forever.

Was it worth it?

For the son it was. Artful Eddie's boy lived up to the sacrifice. His is one of the best-known names in the world.

But before we talk about the son, let's talk about the principle: risky love. Love that takes a chance. Love that goes out on a limb. Love that makes a statement and leaves a legacy. Sacrificial love.

Love that is unexpected, surprising, and stirring. Acts of love that steal the heart and leave impressions on the soul. Acts of love that are never forgotten.

Such an act of love was seen in the last week of the life of Jesus. A demonstration of devotion that the world will never forget. An act of extravagant tenderness in which Jesus wasn't the giver; he was the receiver.

A cluster of friends encircle Jesus. They are at the table. The city is Bethany and the house is Simon's.

He was known as Simon the leper. But not any longer. Now he is just Simon. We don't know when Jesus healed him. But we do know what he was like before Jesus healed him. Stooped shoulders. Fingerless hand. Scabbed arm and infected back draped in rags. A tattered wrap that hides all of the face except for two screaming white eyes.

But that was before Jesus' touch. Was Simon the one Jesus healed after he delivered the Sermon on the Mount? Was he the one in the ten who returned to say thank you? Was he one of the four thousand Jesus helped in Bethsaida? Or was he one of the nameless myriads the gospel writers didn't take time to mention?

We don't know. But we know he had Jesus and his disciples over for dinner.

A simple act, but it must have meant a lot to Jesus. After all, the Pharisees are already clearing him a cell on death row. Won't be long until they finger Lazarus as an accomplice. Could be that the whole lot of them will be on wanted posters by the end of the week. It takes nerve to have a wanted man in your home.

But it takes more nerve to put your hand on a leper's sore.

Simon didn't forget what Jesus had done. He couldn't forget. Where there had been a nub, there was now a finger for his daughter to hold. Where there had been ulcerous sores, there was now skin for his wife to stroke. And where there had been lonely hours in quarantine, there were now happy hours such as this—a house full of friends, a table full of food.

No, Simon didn't forget. Simon knew what it was like to stare death in the face. He knew what it was like to have no home to call your own, and he knew what it was like to be misunderstood. He wanted Jesus to know that if he ever needed a meal and a place to lay his head, there was one house in Bethany to which he could go.

Other homes will not be as gracious as Simon's. Before the week is up, Jesus will spend some time in the high priest's house, the nicest in Jerusalem. Three barns in the back and a beautiful view of the valley. But Jesus won't see the view; he'll see only the false witnesses, hear the lies, and feel the slaps on his face.

He won't find hospitality in the home of the high priest.

Before the week is up, Jesus will visit the chambers of Herod. Elegant chambers. Plenty of servants. Perhaps there is fruit and wine on the table. But Herod won't offer any to Jesus. Herod wants a trick. A sideshow. "Show me a miracle, country boy," he will jab. The guards will snicker.

Before the week is up, Jesus will visit the home of Pilate. Rare opportunity to stand before the couch of the procurator of all Israel. Should be an honor. Should be a moment to remember, but it won't be. It's a moment the world would rather forget. Pilate has an opportunity to perform the world's greatest act of mercy—and he doesn't. God is in his house and Pilate doesn't see him.

We can't help but wonder, *What if?* What if Pilate had come to the defense of the innocent? What if Herod had asked Jesus for help and not entertainment? What if the high priest had been as concerned with truth as he was his position? What if one of them had turned his back on the crowd and his face toward the Christ and made a stand?

But no one did. The mountain of prestige was too high. The fall would have been too great.

But Simon did. Risky love seizes the moment. Simon took a chance. He gave Jesus a good meal. Not much, but more than most. And when the priests accused and the soldiers slapped, perhaps Jesus remembered what Simon did and was strengthened.

And when he remembered Simon's meal, perhaps he remembered Mary's gesture. Maybe he could even smell the perfume.

Not unlikely that he could. After all, it was twelve ounces' worth.

Imported. Concentrated. Sweet. Strong enough to scent a man's clothes for days.

Between the lashings, I wonder, did he relive the moment? As he hugged the Roman post and braced himself for the next ripping of his back, did he remember the oil that soothed his skin? Could he, in the faces of the women who stared, see the small, soft face of Mary, who cared?

She was the only one who believed him. Whenever he spoke of his death the others shrugged, the others doubted, but Mary believed. Mary believed because he spoke with a firmness she'd heard before.

"Lazarus, come out!" he'd demanded, and her brother came out. After four days in a stone-sealed grave he walked out.

And as Mary kissed the now-warm hands of her just-dead brother, she turned and looked. Jesus was smiling. Tear streaks were dry and the teeth shone from beneath the beard. He was smiling.

And in her heart she knew she would never doubt his words.

So when he spoke of his death, she believed.

And when she saw the three together, she couldn't resist. Simon, the healed leper, head thrown back in laughter. Lazarus, the resurrected corpse, leaning in to see what Jesus has said. And Jesus, the source of life for both, beginning his joke a second time.

"Now is the right time," she told herself.

It wasn't an act of impulse. She'd carried the large vial of perfume from her house to Simon's. It wasn't a spontaneous gesture. But it was an extravagant one. The perfume was worth a year's wages. Maybe the only thing of value she had. It wasn't a logical thing to do, but since when has love been led by logic?

Logic hadn't touched Simon.

Common sense hadn't wept at Lazarus's tomb.

Practicality didn't feed the crowds or love the children. Love did. Extravagant, risky, chance-taking love.

And now someone needs to show the same to the giver of such love.

So Mary did. She stepped up behind him and stood with the jar in her hand. Within a couple of moments every mouth was silent and every eye wide as they watched her nervous fingers remove the ornate cover.

Only Jesus was unaware of her presence. Just as he noticed everyone looking behind him, she began to pour. Over his head. Over his shoulders. Down his back. She would have poured herself out for him if she could.

The fragrance rushed through the room. Smells of cooked lamb and herbs were lost in the aroma of the sweet ointment.

"Wherever you go," the gesture spoke, "breathe the aroma and remember one who cares."

On his skin the fragrance of faith. In his clothing the balm of belief. Even as the soldiers divided his garments, her gesture brought a bouquet into a cemetery.

The other disciples had mocked her extravagance. They thought it foolish. Ironic. Jesus had saved them from a sinking boat in a stormy sea. He'd enabled them to heal and preach. He'd brought focus into their fuzzy lives. They, the recipients of exorbitant love, chastised her generosity.

"Why waste that perfume? It could have been sold for a great deal of money that could be given to the poor," they smirk.

Don't miss Jesus' prompt defense of Mary: "Why are you troubling this woman? She did an excellent thing for me" (Matt. 26:10).[1]

Jesus' message is just as powerful today as it was then. Don't miss it: "There is a time for risky love. There is a time for extravagant gestures. There is a time to pour out your affections on one you love. And when the time comes—seize it, don't miss it."

The young husband is packing his wife's belongings. His task solemn. His heart heavy. He never dreamed she would die so young. But the cancer came so surely, so quickly. At the bottom of the drawer he finds a box, a negligee. Unworn. Still wrapped in paper. "She was always waiting for a special occasion," he says to himself, "always waiting . . ."

As the boy on the bicycle watches the students taunt, he churns inside. That's his little brother they are laughing at. He knows he should step in and stand up for his brother, but . . . those are his friends doing the teasing. What will they think? And because it matters what they think, he turns and pedals away.

As the husband looks in the jewelry case, he rationalizes, "Sure she would want the watch, but it's too expensive. She's a practical woman; she'll understand. I'll just get the bracelet today. I'll buy the watch . . . someday."

Someday. The enemy of risky love is a snake whose tongue has mastered the talk of deception. "Someday," he hisses.

"Someday, I can take her on the cruise."

"Someday, I will have time to call and chat."

"Someday, the children will understand why I was so busy."

But you know the truth, don't you? You know even before I write it. You could say it better than I.

Some days never come.

And the price of practicality is sometimes higher than extravagance.

But the rewards of risky love are always greater than its cost.

Go to the effort. Invest the time. Write the letter. Make the apology. Take the trip. Purchase the gift. Do it. The seized opportunity renders joy. The neglected brings regret.

The reward was great for Simon. He was privileged to give rest to the one who made the earth. Simon's gesture will never be forgotten.

Neither will Mary's. Jesus promised, "Wherever the Good News is preached in all the world, what this woman has done will be told, and people will remember her" (v. 13).

Simon and Mary: examples of the risky gift given at the right time.

Which brings us back to Artful Eddie, the Chicago mobster who squealed on Al Capone so his son could have a fair chance. Had Eddie lived to see his son Butch grow up, he would have been proud.

He would have been proud of Butch's appointment to Annapolis. He would have been proud of the commissioning as a World War II navy pilot. He would have been proud as he read of his son downing five bombers in the Pacific night and saving the lives of hundreds of crew-men on the carrier *Lexington*. The name was cleared. The Congressional Medal of Honor that Butch received was proof.

When people say the name O'Hare in Chicago, they don't think gangsters—they think aviation heroism. And now when you say his name, you have something else to think about. Think about the undy-ing dividends of risky love. Think about it the next time you hear it. Think about it the next time you fly into the airport named after the son of a gangster gone good.

The son of Eddie O'Hare.

QUESTIONS FOR REFLECTION AND DISCUSSION

1. Describe your initial reaction to Mary's action. Did you think it foolish? Exorbitant? Profound? Moving?

2. What are the appropriate times for risky love? Describe them. When have you chosen to demonstrate risky love? What was the outcome? Would you do it again? Why?

3. In what way does practicality sometimes cost more than extravagance? Do you agree that "the rewards of risky love are always greater than its cost"? Why or why not?

4. Read Matthew 26:6–13. In what way was the woman's action a beautiful thing? How was it symbolic of what was to happen? Why do you suppose Jesus said what he did in verse 13?

5. Max writes, "The seized opportunity renders joy. The neglected brings regret." What opportunities exist for you right now to show risky love? List them. What's stopping you from taking the risk?

Chapter 3

❧

JACOB

During the night Jacob rose and crossed the Jabbok River at the crossing, taking with him his two wives, his two slave girls, and his eleven sons. He sent his family and everything he had across the river. So Jacob was alone, and a man came and wrestled with him until the sun came up. When the man saw he could not defeat Jacob, he struck Jacob's hip and put it out of joint.

Then he said to Jacob, "Let me go. The sun is coming up."

But Jacob said, "I will let you go if you will bless me."

The man said to him, "What is your name?"

And he answered, "Jacob."

Then the man said, "Your name will no longer be Jacob. Your name will now be Israel, because you have wrestled with God and with people, and you have won."

Then Jacob asked him, "Please tell me your name."

But the man said, "Why do you ask my name?" Then he blessed Jacob there.

So Jacob named that place Peniel, saying, "I have seen God face to face, but my life was saved."

— GENESIS 32:22–30

WRESTLING WITH THE PAST

He was the riverboat gambler of the patriarchs. A master of sleight of hand and fancy footwork. He had gained a seamy reputation of getting what he wanted by hook or crook—or both.

Twice he dealt hidden cards to his dull-witted brother Esau in order to climb the family tree. He once pulled the wool over the eyes of his own father, a trick especially dirty since his father's eyes were rather dim, and the wool he pulled ensured him a gift he would never have received otherwise.

He later conned his father-in-law out of his best livestock and, when no one was looking, he took the kids and the cattle and skedaddled.

Yes, Jacob had a salty reputation, deservedly so. For him the ends always justified the means. His cleverness was outranked only by his audacity. His conscience was calloused just enough to let him sleep and his feet were just fast enough to keep him one step ahead of the consequences.

That is, until he reached a river called Jabbok (Genesis 32). At Jabbok his own cunning caught up with him.

Jacob was camped near the river Jabbok when word reached him that big, hairy Esau was coming to see him. It had been twenty years since Jacob had tricked his brother. More than enough time, Jacob realized, for Esau to stir up a boiling pot of revenge. Jacob was in trouble. This time he had no more tricks up his sleeve. He was finally forced to face up to himself and to God.

To Jacob's credit, he didn't run away from the problem. One has to wonder why. Maybe he was sick of running. Or maybe he was tired of looking at the shady character he saw every morning in the mirror. Or maybe he simply knew that he'd dealt from the bottom of the deck one too many times. Whatever the motivation, it was enough to cause him to come out of the shadows, cross Jabbok Creek alone, and face the facts.

The word *Jabbok* in Hebrew means "wrestle," and wrestle is what Jacob did. He wrestled with his past: all the white lies, scheming, and scandalizing. He wrestled with his situation: a spider trapped in his own web of deceit and craftiness. But more than anything, he wrestled with God.

He wrestled with the same God who had descended the ladder at Bethel to assure Jacob he wasn't alone (although he deserved to be). He met the same God who had earlier guaranteed Jacob that he would never break his promise (though one could hardly fault God if he did). He confronted the same God who had reminded Jacob that the land prepared for him was still his. (Proof again that God blesses us *in spite* of our lives and not *because of* our lives.)

Jacob wrestled with God the entire night. On the banks of Jabbok he rolled in the mud of his mistakes. He met God face-to-face, sick of his past and in desperate need of a fresh start. And because Jacob wanted it so badly, God honored his determination. God gave him a new name and a new promise. But he also gave a wrenched hip as a reminder of that mysterious night at the river.

Jacob wasn't the only man in the Bible to wrestle with self and God because of past antics. David did after his rendezvous with Bathsheba. Samson wrestled, blind and bald after Delilah's seduction. Elijah was at his own Jabbok when he heard the "still small voice" (1 Kings 19:12 NKJV). Peter wrestled with his guilt with echoes of a crowing cock still ringing in his ears.

And I imagine that most of us have spent some time on the riverbanks as well. Our scandalous deeds have a way of finding us. Want some examples? Consider these scenes.

The unfaithful husband standing at the table with a note from his wife in his hands: "I couldn't take it anymore. I've taken the kids with me."

The twenty-year-old single woman in the doctor's office. The words are still fresh on her mind: "The test was positive. You are pregnant."

The businessman squirming in the IRS office. "Your audit shows that you took some loopholes that weren't yours to take."

The red-faced student who got caught red-handed copying the test answers of someone else. "We'll have to notify your parents."

All of us at one time or another come face-to-face with our past. And it's always an awkward encounter. When our sins catch up with us we can do one of two things: run or wrestle.

Many choose to run. They brush it off with a shrug of rationalization. "I was a victim of circumstances." Or, "It was his fault." Or, "There are many who do worse things." The problem with this escape is that it's no escape at all. It's only a shallow camouflage. No matter how many layers of makeup you put over a black eye, underneath it is still black. And down deep it still hurts.

Jacob finally figured that out. As a result, his example is one worthy of imitation. The best way to deal with our past is to hitch up our pants, roll up our sleeves, and face it head-on. No more buck-passing or scapegoating. No more glossing over or covering up. No more games. We need a confrontation with our Master.

We, too, should cross the creek alone and struggle with God over ourselves. We, too, should stand eyeball to eyeball with him and be reminded that left alone we fail. We, too, should unmask our stained hearts and grimy souls and be honest with the one who knows our most secret sins.

The result could be refreshing. We know it was for Jacob. After his encounter with God, Jacob was a new man. He crossed the river in the dawn of a new day and faced Esau with newfound courage.

Each step he took, however, was a painful one. His stiff hip was a reminder of the lesson he had learned at Jabbok: shady dealings bring pain. Mark it down: play today and tomorrow you'll pay.

And for you who wonder if you've played too long to change, take courage from Jacob's legacy. No man is too bad for God. To transform a riverboat gambler into a man of faith would be no easy task. But for God, it was all in a night's work.

QUESTIONS FOR REFLECTION AND DISCUSSION

1. What happens when we try to ignore the past? What does Max mean by "The best way to deal with our past is to hitch up our pants, roll up our sleeves, and face it head-on"? How is that different from dwelling on the past?

2. Read Genesis 32:1–33:3. Why did Jacob fear meeting Esau again? How did Jacob face the situation head-on?

3. How can we wrestle with God in dealing with our past? In what way might we also carry a limp?

4. Have you ever talked with someone who believed he or she had lived too bad a life to be accepted by God? What did you say to that person?

5. At the end of Jacob's life, what promise does God make to Jacob in Genesis 46:2–4? What blessings came through the descendants of Jacob?

Chapter 4

❦

CORNELIUS

God has shown me that he doesn't think anyone is unclean or unfit.

—ACTS 10:28 CEV

STABLE THE HIGH HORSE

Molokai, a ruby on the pearl necklace of the Hawaiian Islands. Tourists travel to Molokai for its quiet charm, gentle breezes, and soft surf. But Father Damien came for a different reason. He came to help people die.

He came to Molokai because leprosy came here first. No one knows exactly how the disease reached Hawaii. The first documented case was dated around 1840. But while no one can trace the source of the disease, no one can deny its results. Disfigurement, decay, and panic.

The government responded with a civil version of Old Testament segregation. They deposited the diseased on a triangular thrust of land called Kalaupapa. Surrounded on three sides by water and on the fourth by the highest seawall in the world, it was a natural prison.

Hard to get to. Harder still to get away from.

The lepers lived a discarded existence in shanties with minimal food. Ships would draw close to shore, and sailors would dump supplies into the water, hoping the crates would float toward land. Society sent the lepers a clear message: you aren't valuable anymore.

But Father Damien's message was different. He'd already served in the islands for a decade when, in 1873, at the age of thirty-three, he wrote his provincial and offered, "I want to sacrifice myself for the poor lepers."

He immersed himself in their world, dressing sores, hugging children, burying the dead. His choir members sang through rags, and congregants received communion with stumped hands. Because they mattered to God, they mattered to him. When he referred to his congregation, he didn't say "my brothers and sisters" but "we lepers." He became one of them. Literally.

Somewhere along the way, through a touch of kindness or in the sharing of a communion wafer, the disease passed from member to priest. Damien became a leper. And on April 15, 1889, four days shy of Good Friday, he died.[1]

We've learned to treat leprosy. We don't quarantine people anymore. We've done away with such settlements. But have we done away with the attitude? Do we still see some people as inferior?

We did on our elementary school playground. All the boys in Mrs. Amburgy's first-grade class bonded together to express our male superiority. We met daily at recess and, with arms interlocked, marched around the playground, shouting, "Boys are better than girls! Boys are better than girls!" Frankly, I didn't agree, but I enjoyed the fraternity. The girls, in response, formed their own club. They paraded around the school, announcing their disdain for boys. We were a happy campus.

People are prone to pecking orders. We love the high horse. The boy over the girl or girl over boy. The affluent over the destitute. The educated over the dropout. The old-timer over the newcomer. The Jew over the Gentile.

An impassable gulf yawned between Jews and Gentiles in the days of the early church. A Jew could not drink milk drawn by Gentiles or eat their food. Jews could not aid a Gentile mother in her hour of need. Jewish physicians could not attend to non-Jewish patients.[2]

No Jew would have anything to do with a Gentile. They were unclean.

Unless that Jew, of course, was Jesus. Suspicions of a new order began to surface because of his curious conversation with the Canaanite woman. Her daughter was dying, and her prayer was urgent. Yet her ancestry was Gentile. "I was sent only to help God's lost sheep—the people of Israel," Jesus told her. "That's true, Lord," she replied, "but even dogs are allowed to eat the scraps that fall beneath their masters' table" (Matt. 15:24, 27 NLT 2007).

Jesus healed the woman's daughter and made his position clear. He was more concerned about bringing everyone in than shutting certain people out.

This was the tension Peter felt. His culture said, "Keep your distance from Gentiles." His Christ said, "Build bridges to Gentiles." And Peter had to make a choice. An encounter with Cornelius forced his decision.

Cornelius was an officer in the Roman army. Both Gentile and bad guy. (Think British redcoat in eighteenth-century Boston.) He ate the wrong food, hung with the wrong crowd, and swore allegiance to Caesar. He didn't quote the Torah or descend from Abraham. Toga on his body and ham in his freezer. No yarmulke on his head or beard on his face. Hardly deacon material. Uncircumcised, unkosher, unclean. Look at him.

Yet look at him again. Closely. He helped needy people and sympathized with Jewish ethics. He was kind and devout. "One who feared God with all his household, who gave alms generously to the people, and prayed to God always" (Acts 10:2 NKJV). Cornelius was even on a first-name basis with an angel. The angel told him to get in touch with Peter, who was staying at a friend's house thirty miles away in the seaside town of Joppa. Cornelius sent three men to find him.

Peter, meanwhile, was doing his best to pray with a growling stomach. "He became very hungry and wanted to eat; but while they made ready, he fell into a trance and saw heaven opened and an object like a great sheet bound at the four corners, descending to him and let down to the earth. In it were all kinds of four-footed animals of the earth, wild beasts, creeping things, and birds of the air. And a voice came to him, 'Rise, Peter; kill and eat'" (vv. 10–13 NKJV).

The sheet contained enough unkosher food to uncurl the payos of any Hasidic Jew. Peter absolutely and resolutely refused. "Not so, Lord! For I have never eaten anything common or unclean" (v. 14 NKJV).

But God wasn't kidding about this. He three-peated the vision, leaving poor Peter in a quandary. Peter was pondering the pigs in the blanket when he heard a knock at the door. At the sound of the knock, he heard the call of God's Spirit in his heart. "Behold, three men are seeking you. Arise therefore, go down and go with them, doubting nothing; for I have sent them" (vv. 19–20 NKJV).

"Doubting nothing" can also be translated "make no distinction" or "indulge in no prejudice" or "discard all partiality." This was a huge moment for Peter.

Much to his credit, Peter invited the messengers to spend the night and headed out the next morning to meet Cornelius. When Peter arrived, Cornelius fell at his feet. Peter insisted he stand up and then confessed how difficult this decision had been. "You know that we Jews are not allowed to have anything to do with other people. But God has shown me that he doesn't think anyone is unclean or unfit" (v. 28 CEV).

Peter told Cornelius about Jesus and the gospel, and before Peter could issue an invitation, the presence of the Spirit was among them, and they were replicating Pentecost—speaking in tongues and glorifying God. Peter offered to baptize Cornelius and his friends. They accepted. They offered him a bed. Peter accepted. By the end of the visit, he was making his own ham sandwiches.

And us? We are still pondering verse 28: "God has shown me that he doesn't think anyone is unclean or unfit."

Life is so much easier without this command. As long as we can call people common or unfit, we can plant them on Kalaupapa and go our separate ways. Labels relieve us of responsibility. Pigeonholing permits us to wash our hands and leave.

"Oh, I know John. He is an alcoholic." (Translation: "Why can't he control himself?")

"The new boss is a liberal Democrat." (Translation: "Can't he see how misguided he is?")

"Oh, I know her. She's divorced." (Translation: "She has a lot of baggage.")

Categorizing others creates distance and gives us a convenient exit strategy for avoiding involvement.

Jesus took an entirely different approach. He was all about including people, not excluding them. "The Word became flesh and blood, and moved into the neighborhood" (John 1:14 MSG). Jesus touched lepers and loved foreigners and spent so much time with partygoers that people called him a "lush, a friend of the riffraff" (Matt. 11:19 MSG).

Racism couldn't keep him from the Samaritan woman; demons couldn't keep him from the demoniac. His Facebook page included the likes of Zacchaeus the Ponzi-meister, Matthew the IRS agent, and some floozy he met at Simon's house. Jesus spent thirty-three years walking in the mess of this world. "He had equal status with God but didn't think so much of himself that he had to cling to the advantages of that status no matter what. Not at all. When the time came, he set aside the privileges of deity and took on the status of a slave, became *human!*" (Phil. 2:6–7 MSG; emphasis added).

His example sends this message: no playground displays of superiority. "Don't call any person common or unfit."

My friend Roosevelt would agree. He is a leader in our congregation and one of the nicest guys in the history of humanity. He lives next door to a single mom who was cited by their homeowners' association for an unkempt lawn. A jungle of overgrown bushes and untrimmed trees obscured her house. The association warned her to get her yard cleaned up. The warning was followed by a police officer's visit. The officer gave her two weeks to do the work or appear in court. Her yard was a blight on the street, maybe even a health hazard.

Roosevelt, however, paid his neighbor, Terry, a visit. There is always a story behind the door, and he found a sad one. She had just weathered a rough divorce, was recovering from surgery, and was working a night shift at the hospital and extra hours to make ends meet. Her only son was stationed in Iraq. Terry was in survival mode: alone, sick, and exhausted. Lawn care? The least of her concerns.

So Roosevelt recruited several neighbors, and the families spent a Saturday morning getting things in order. They cut shrubs and branches and carted out a dozen bags of leaves. A few days later Terry sent this message to the board of the homeowners' association:

Dear Sirs,

I am hoping that you can make the neighborhood aware of what a great group of neighbors I have. These neighbors unselfishly toiled in my yard.

Their actions encouraged and reminded me that there are still some compassionate people residing here, people who care enough to reach out to strangers in their times of need to help lessen their burdens. These residents are to be commended, and I cannot adequately express how grateful I am for their hard work, positive attitude, and enthusiasm. This is all the more amazing considering my grandfather was a rabbi, and I have a mezuzah at my front door!

Roosevelt's response was a Christlike response. Rather than see people as problems, Christ saw them as opportunities.

May we consider a few more Cornelius moments?

You and your buddies enter the cafeteria, carrying your lunch trays. As you take your seat at the table, one of the guys elbows you and says, "Get a load of the new kid." You have no trouble spotting him. He's the only student wearing a turban. Your friend makes this wisecrack: "Still wearing his towel from the shower."

You might have made a joke yourself, except yesterday your pastor shared the story of Peter and Cornelius and read this verse: "God has shown me that he doesn't think anyone is unclean or unfit" (Acts 10:28 CEV).

Hmm.

The guy in the next cubicle wears boots, chews tobacco, and drives a truck with a rifle rack. You wear loafers, eat health food, and drive a hybrid, except on Fridays when you pedal your bike to work. He makes racist jokes. Doesn't he notice that you are black? He has a rebel flag as a screen saver. Your great-grandfather was a slave. You'd love to distance yourself from this redneck.

Yet this morning's Bible study included this challenge: "God has shown me that he doesn't think anyone is unclean or unfit" (v. 28 CEV).

Now what do you do?

One more. You are the superintendent of an orphanage. In dealing with the birth certificates, you come across a troubling word: *illegitimate*. As you research further, you learn that the word is a permanent label, never to be removed from the certificate.

This is what Edna Gladney discovered. And she couldn't bear the thought of it. If *legitimate* means to be legal, lawful, and valid, what does *illegitimate* mean? Can you imagine living with such a label?

Mrs. Gladney couldn't. It took her three years, but in 1936 she successfully lobbied the Texas legislature to remove the term from birth documents.[3]

God calls us to change the way we look at people. Not to see them as Gentiles or Jews, insiders or outsiders, liberals or conservatives. Not to label. To label is to libel. "We have stopped evaluating others from a human point of view" (2 Cor. 5:16 NLT 2007).

Let's view people differently; let's view them as we do ourselves. Blemished, perhaps. Unfinished, for certain. Yet once rescued and restored, we may shed light, like the two stained-glass windows in my office.

My brother found them on a junkyard heap. Some church had discarded them. Dee, a handy carpenter, reclaimed them. He repainted the chipped wood, repaired the worn frame. He sealed some of the cracks in the colored glass. The windows aren't perfect. But if suspended where the sun can pass through, they cascade multicolored light into the room.

In our lifetimes you and I are going to come across some discarded people. Tossed out. Sometimes tossed out by a church. And we get to choose. Neglect or rescue? Label them or love them? We know Jesus' choice. Just look at what he did with us.

QUESTIONS FOR REFLECTION AND DISCUSSION

1. What was the social pecking order when you were growing up? How about today? Who is at the top, who is at the bottom, and where are you in the order?

2. In what situations do you hear offensive labeling? Have you found yourself inadvertently following suit? How can you be a leader of change in this environment?

3. Recall a time when you were in a situation similar to that of Peter in Acts 10. When have the customs or behaviors of another culture or race felt uncomfortable or even offensive to you? What would be your reaction if God called you to take up the habits and practices of another group so you could reach out to them?

4. Why did Cornelius not look the part even though he was a Christ follower? What surface judgments do people use today to measure spirituality?

5. How could you make time for some marginalized Christians in your life?

Chapter 5

THE WOMAN WITH THE ISSUE OF BLOOD

A large crowd followed Jesus and pushed very close around him. Among them was a woman who had been bleeding for twelve years. She had suffered very much from many doctors and had spent all the money she had, but instead of improving, she was getting worse. When the woman heard about Jesus, she came up behind him in the crowd and touched his coat. She thought, "If I can just touch his clothes, I will be healed." Instantly her bleeding stopped, and she felt in her body that she was healed from her disease.

At once Jesus felt power go out from him. So he turned around in the crowd and asked, "Who touched my clothes?"

His followers said, "Look at how many people are pushing against you! And you ask, 'Who touched me?'"

But Jesus continued looking around to see who had touched him. The woman, knowing that she was healed, came and fell at Jesus' feet. Shaking with fear, she told him the whole truth. Jesus said to her, "Dear woman, you are made well because you believed. Go in peace; be healed of your disease."

—MARK 5:24–34

A Crazy Hunch and
a High Hope

A clock for Christmas is not the kind of gift that thrills an eight-year-old boy, but I said thank you and took it to my bedroom, put it on the nightstand, and plugged it in.

It was a square-faced Bulova. It didn't have moving numbers—it had rotating hands. It didn't play tapes or CDs, but over the years it developed a slight, soothing hum that could be heard when the room was quiet.

Today you can buy clocks that sound like rain when it's time to sleep and like your mother when it's time to wake up. But not this one. Its alarm could make the dogs howl. Forget snooze buttons. Just pick it up and chuck it across the room. It was a Neanderthal model. It wouldn't net fifty cents at a garage sale in this day of digital clocks and musical alarms.

But still, over time, I grew attached to it. People don't usually get sentimental about electric clocks, but I did about this one. Not because of its accuracy; it was always a bit slow. Nor the hum, which I didn't mind. I liked it because of the light.

You see, this clock glowed in the dark.

All day, every day it soaked up the light. It sponged up the sun. The hands were little sticks of ticks and time and sunshine. And when the night came, the clock was ready. When I flicked off the light to sleep, the little clock flicked on its light and shined. Not much light, but when your world is dark, just a little seems like a lot.

Somewhat like the light a woman got when she met Jesus.

We don't know her name, but we know her situation. Her world was midnight black. Grope-in-the-dark-and-hope-for-help black. Read these three verses and see what I mean:

A large crowd followed Jesus and pushed very close around him. Among them was a woman who had been bleeding for twelve years. She had suffered very much from many doctors and had spent all the money she had, but instead of improving, she was getting worse. (Mark 5:24–26)

She was a bruised reed: "bleeding for twelve years," "suffered very much," "spent all the money she had," and "getting worse."

A chronic menstrual disorder. A perpetual issue of blood. Such a condition would be difficult for any woman of any era. But for a Jewess, nothing could be worse. No part of her life was left unaffected.

Sexually . . . she could not touch her husband.

Maternally . . . she could not bear children.

Domestically . . . anything she touched was considered unclean.

No washing dishes. No sweeping floors.

Spiritually . . . she was not allowed to enter the temple.

She was physically exhausted and socially ostracized.

She had sought help "under the care of many doctors" (v. 26 NIV). The Talmud gives no fewer than eleven cures for such a condition. No doubt she had tried them all. Some were legitimate treatments. Others, such as carrying the ashes of an ostrich egg in a linen cloth, were hollow superstitions.

She "had spent all she had" (v. 26 NIV). To dump financial strain on top of the physical strain is to add insult to injury. A friend battling cancer told me that the hounding of the creditors who demand payments for ongoing medical treatment is just as devastating as the pain.

"Instead of getting better she grew worse" (v. 26 NIV). She was a bruised reed. She awoke daily in a body that no one wanted. She is down to her last prayer. And on the day we encounter her, she's about to pray it.

By the time she gets to Jesus, he is surrounded by people. He's on his way to help the daughter of Jairus, the most important man in the community. What are the odds that he will interrupt an urgent mission with a high official to help the likes of her? Very few. But what are the odds that she will survive if she doesn't take a chance? Fewer still. So she takes a chance.

"If I can just touch his clothes," she thinks, "I will be healed" (v. 28).

Risky decision. To touch him, she will have to touch the people. If one of them recognizes her . . . hello rebuke, good-bye cure. But what choice does she have? She has no money, no clout, no friends, no solutions. All she has is a crazy hunch that Jesus can help and a high hope that he will.

Maybe that's all you have: a crazy hunch and a high hope. You have nothing to give. But you are hurting. And all you have to offer him is your hurt.

Maybe that has kept you from coming to God. Oh, you've taken a step or two in his direction. But then you saw the other people around him. They seemed so clean, so neat, so trim and fit in their faith. And when you saw them, they blocked your view of him. So you stepped back.

If that describes you, note carefully, only one person was commended that day for having faith. It wasn't a wealthy giver. It wasn't a loyal follower. It wasn't an acclaimed teacher. It was a shame-struck, penniless outcast who clutched onto her hunch that he could and her hope that he would.

Which, by the way, isn't a bad definition of faith: *A conviction that he can and a hope that he will.* Sounds similar to the definition of faith given by the Bible. "Without faith no one can please God. Anyone who comes to God must believe that he is real and that he rewards those who truly want to find him" (Heb. 11:6).

Not too complicated, is it? Faith is the belief that God is real and that God is good. Faith is not a mystical experience or a midnight vision or a voice in the forest . . . it is a choice to believe that the one who made it all hasn't left it all and that he still sends light into shadows and responds to gestures of faith.

There was no guarantee, of course. She hoped he'd respond . . . she longed for it . . . but she didn't know if he would. All she knew was that he was there and that he was good. That's faith.

Faith is not the belief that God will do what you want. Faith is the belief that God will do what is right.

"Blessed are the dirt-poor, nothing-to-give, trapped-in-a-corner, destitute, diseased," Jesus said, "for theirs is the kingdom of heaven" (Matt. 5:6; my translation).

God's economy is upside down (or right side up and ours is upside down!). God says that the more hopeless your circumstance, the more likely your salvation. The greater your cares, the more genuine your prayers. The darker the room, the greater the need for light.

Which takes us back to my clock. When it was daylight, I never appreciated my little Bulova's capacity to glow in the dark. But as the shadows grew, so did my gratitude.

A healthy lady never would have appreciated the power of a touch of the hem of his robe. But this woman was sick . . . and when her dilemma met his dedication, a miracle occurred.

Her part in the healing was very small. All she did was extend her arm through the crowd.

"If only I can touch him."

What's important is not the form of the effort but the fact of the effort. The fact is, she did something. She refused to settle for sickness another day and resolved to make a move.

Healing begins when we do something. Healing begins when we reach out. Healing starts when we take a step.

God's help is near and always available, but it is only given to those who seek it. Nothing results from apathy. The great work in this story is the mighty healing that occurred. But the great truth is that the healing began with her touch. And with that small, courageous gesture, she experienced Jesus' tender power.

Compared to God's part, our part is minuscule but necessary. We don't have to do much, *but we do have to do something.*

Write a letter.

Ask forgiveness.

Call a counselor.

Confess.

Call Mom.

Visit a doctor.

Be baptized.

Feed a hungry person.

Pray.

Teach.

Go.

Do something that demonstrates faith. For faith with no effort is no faith at all. *God will respond*. He has never rejected a genuine gesture of faith. Never.

God honors radical, risk-taking faith.

When arks are built, lives are saved. When soldiers march, Jerichos tumble. When staffs are raised, seas still open. When a lunch is shared, thousands are fed. And when a garment is touched—whether by the hand of an anemic woman in Galilee or by the prayers of a beggar in Bangladesh—Jesus stops. He stops and responds.

Mark can tell you. When this woman touched Christ, two things happened that happen nowhere else in the Bible. He recorded them both.

First, Jesus heals before he knows it. The power left automatically and instantaneously. It's as if the Father short-circuited the system and the divinity of Christ was a step ahead of the humanity of Christ.

Her need summoned his help. No neon lights or loud shouts. No razzle-dazzle. No fanfare. No hoopla. No splash. Just help.

Just like my dark room brought the light out of my clock, our dark world brings out the light of God.

Second, he calls her *daughter*. "Daughter, your faith has made you well" (v. 34 NKJV). It's the only time Jesus calls *any* woman *anywhere* daughter. Imagine how that made her feel! Who could remember the last time she received a term of affection? Who knew the last time kind eyes had met hers?

Leo Tolstoy, the great Russian writer, told of the time he was walking down the street and passed a beggar. Tolstoy reached into his pocket to give the beggar some money, but his pocket was empty. Tolstoy turned to the man and said, "I'm sorry, my brother, but I have nothing to give."

The beggar brightened and said, "You have given me more than I asked for—you have called me brother."

To the loved, a word of affection is a morsel, but to the love-starved, a word of affection can be a feast.

And Jesus gave this woman a banquet.

Tradition holds that she never forgot what Jesus did. Legend states that she stayed with Jesus and followed him as he carried his cross up Calvary. Some believe she was Veronica, the woman who walked the road to the cross with him. And when the sweat and blood were stinging his eyes, she wiped his forehead.

She, at an hour of great need, received his touch—and he, at an hour of pain, received hers. We don't know if the legend is true, but we know it could be. And I don't know if the same has happened to you, but I know it can.

QUESTIONS FOR REFLECTION AND DISCUSSION

1. What was the crazy hunch and the high hope of the woman in Mark 5? In specific terms, how can she be an example for us today?
2. Discuss Max's definition of faith: "A conviction that [God] can and a hope that he will."
3. Max writes, "Faith is not the belief that God will do what you want. Faith is the belief that God will do what is right." How should this change the way you pray? Why?
4. Is it true that "faith with no effort is no faith at all"? Explain your answer.
5. What is significant about the fact that Jesus called the afflicted woman "daughter"? Does this mean anything for your relationship with Jesus?

Chapter 6

PHILIP

The eunuch said, "See, here is water. What hinders me from being baptized?" Then Philip said, "If you believe with all your heart, you may."

—ACTS 8:36–37 NKJV

BLAST A FEW WALLS

Fans rooted for the competition. Cheerleaders switched loyalties. The coach helped the opposition score points. Parents yelled for the competition.

What was this?

This was the brainchild of a big-hearted football coach in Grapevine, Texas. Kris Hogan skippers the successful program of Faith Christian High School. He has seventy players, eleven coaches, quality equipment, and parents who care, make banners, attend pep rallies, and wouldn't miss a game for their own funerals.

They took their 7–2 record into a contest with Gainesville State School. Gainesville's players, by contrast, wear seven-year-old shoulder pads and last decade's helmets and show up at each game wearing handcuffs. Their parents don't watch them play, but twelve uniformed officers do. That's because Gainesville is a maximum-security correctional facility.

The school doesn't have a stadium, cheerleading squad, or half a hope of winning. Gainesville was 0–8 going into the Grapevine game. They'd scored two touchdowns all year.

The whole situation didn't seem fair. So Coach Hogan devised a plan. He asked the fans to step across the field and, for one night only, to cheer for the other side. More than two hundred volunteered.

They formed a forty-yard spirit line. They painted "Go Tornadoes!" on a banner that the Gainesville squad could burst through. They sat on the Gainesville side of the stadium. They even learned the names of Gainesville players so they could yell for individuals.

The prisoners had heard people scream their names but never like this. Gerald, a lineman who will serve three years, said, "People are a little afraid of us when we come to the games. You can see it in their eyes. They're lookin' at us like we're criminals. But these people, they were yellin' for us. By our names!"

After the game the teams gathered in the middle of the field to say a prayer. One of the incarcerated players asked to lead it. Coach Hogan agreed, not knowing what to expect. "Lord," the boy said, "I don't know how this happened, so I don't know how to say thank you, but I never would've known there was so many people in the world that cared about us."

Grapevine fans weren't finished. After the game they waited beside the Gainesville bus to give each player a good-bye gift—burger, fries, candy, soda, a Bible, an encouraging letter, and a round of applause. As their prison bus left the parking lot, the players pressed stunned faces against the windows and wondered what had just hit them.

Here's what hit them: a squad of bigotry-demolition experts. Their assignment? Blast bias into dust. Their weapons? A fusillade of "You still matter" and "Someone still cares." Their mission? Break down barricades that separate God's children from each other.

Do any walls bisect your world? There you stand on one side. And on the other? The person you've learned to disregard, perhaps even disdain. The teen with the tats. The boss with the bucks. The immigrant with the hard-to-understand accent. The person on the opposite side of your political fence. The beggar who sits outside your church every week.

Or the Samaritans outside Jerusalem.

Talk about a wall, ancient and tall. "Jews," as John wrote in his gospel, "refuse to have anything to do with Samaritans" (John 4:9 NLT). The two cultures had hated each other for a thousand years. The feud involved claims of defection, intermarriage, and disloyalty to the temple. Samaritans were blacklisted. Their beds, utensils—even their spittle—were considered unclean. No orthodox Jew would travel into the region. Most Jews would gladly double the length of their trip rather than go through Samaria.

Jesus, however, played by a different set of rules. He spent the better part of a day on the turf of a Samaritan woman, drinking water from her ladle, discussing her questions (John 4:1–26). He stepped across the cultural taboo as if it were a sleeping dog in the doorway. Jesus loves to break down walls.

That's why he sent Philip to Samaria.

> Then Philip went down to the city of Samaria and preached Christ to them. And the multitudes with one accord heeded the things spoken by Philip, hearing and seeing the miracles which he did. For unclean spirits, crying with a loud voice, came out of many who were possessed; and many who were paralyzed and lame were healed. . . .
>
> When they believed Philip as he preached the things concerning the kingdom of God and the name of Jesus Christ, both men and women were baptized. (Acts 8:5–7, 12 NKJV)

The city broke out into a revival. Peter and John heard about the response and traveled from Jerusalem to Samaria to confirm it. "When they had come down, [they] prayed for them that they might receive the Holy Spirit. For as yet He had fallen upon none of them. They had only been baptized in the name of the Lord Jesus. Then they laid hands on them, and they received the Holy Spirit" (vv. 15–17 NKJV).

This is a curious turn of events. Why hadn't the Samaritans received the Holy Spirit? On the Day of Pentecost, Peter promised the gift of the Spirit to those who repented and were baptized. How then can we explain the baptism of the Samaritans, which, according to Luke, was not accompanied by the Spirit? Why delay the gift?

Simple. To celebrate the falling of a wall. The gospel, for the first time, was breaching an ancient bias. God marked the moment with a ticker-tape parade of sorts. He rolled out the welcome mat and sent his apostles to verify the revival and place hands on the Samaritans. Let any doubt be gone: God accepts all people.

But he wasn't finished. He sent Philip on a second cross-cultural mission.

Now an angel of the Lord spoke to Philip, saying, "Arise and go toward the south along the road which goes down from Jerusalem to Gaza." This is desert. So he arose and went. And behold, a man of Ethiopia, a eunuch of great authority under Candace the queen of the Ethiopians, who had charge of all her treasury, and had come to Jerusalem to worship, was returning. And sitting in his chariot, he was reading Isaiah the prophet. Then the Spirit said to Philip, "Go near and overtake this chariot." (vv. 26–29 NKJV)

Walls separated Philip from the eunuch. The Ethiopian was dark skinned; Philip was light. The official hailed from distant Africa; Philip grew up nearby. The traveler was rich enough to travel. And who was Philip but a simple refugee, banished from Jerusalem? And don't overlook the delicate matter of differing testosterone levels. Philip, we later learn, was the father of four girls (Acts 21:9). The official was a eunuch. No wife or kids or plans for either. The lives of the two men could not have been more different.

But Philip didn't hesitate. He "preached Jesus to him. Now as they went down the road, they came to some water. And the eunuch said, 'See, here is water. What hinders me from being baptized?'" (Acts 8:35–36 NKJV).

No small question. A black, influential, effeminate official from Africa turns to the white, simple, virile Christian from Jerusalem and asks, "Is there any reason I can't have what you have?"

What if Philip had said, "Now that you mention it, yes. Sorry. We don't take your type"?

But Philip, charter member of the bigotry-demolition team, blasted through the wall and invited, "'If you believe with all your heart, you may.' And he answered and said, 'I believe that Jesus Christ is the Son of God'" (v. 37 NKJV).

Next thing you know, the eunuch is stepping out of the baptism waters, whistling "Jesus Loves Me," Philip is on to his next assignment, and the church has her first non-Jewish convert.

And we are a bit dizzy. What do we do with a chapter like this? Samaria. Peter and John arriving. Holy Spirit falling. Gaza. Ethiopian official. Philip. What do these events teach us?

They teach us how God feels about the person on the other side of the wall.

He tore down the wall we used to keep each other at a distance. . . . Instead of continuing with two groups of people separated by centuries of animosity and suspicion, he created a new kind of human being, a fresh start for everybody.

Christ brought us together through his death on the cross. The Cross got us to embrace, and that was the end of the hostility. (Eph. 2:14–16 MSG)

The cross of Christ creates a new people, a people unhindered by skin color or family feud. A new citizenry based not on common ancestry or geography but on a common Savior.

My friend Buckner Fanning experienced this firsthand. He was a marine in World War II, stationed in Nagasaki three weeks after the dropping of the atomic bomb. Can you imagine a young American soldier amid the rubble and wreckage of the demolished city? Radiation-burned victims wandering the streets. Atomic fallout showering on the city. Bodies burned to a casket black. Survivors shuffling through the streets, searching for family, food, and hope. The conquering soldier feeling not victory but grief for the suffering around him.

Instead of anger and revenge, Buckner found an oasis of grace. While patrolling the narrow streets, he came upon a sign that bore an English phrase: Methodist Church. He noted the location and resolved to return the next Sunday morning.

When he did, he entered a partially collapsed structure. Windows, shattered. Walls, buckled. The young marine stepped through the rubble, unsure how he would be received.

Fifteen or so Japanese were setting up chairs and removing debris.

When the uniformed American entered their midst, they stopped and turned.

He knew only one word in Japanese. He heard it. *Brother.* "They welcomed me as a friend," Buckner relates, the power of the moment still resonating more than sixty years after the events. They offered him a seat. He opened his Bible and, not understanding the sermon, sat and observed. During Communion the worshippers brought him the elements. In that quiet moment the enmity of their nations and the hurt of the war were set aside as one Christian served another the body and blood of Christ.

Another wall came a-tumblin' down.

What walls are in your world?

Brian Overcast is knocking down walls in Morelia, Mexico. As director of the NOÉ Center (New Opportunities in Education), Brian and his team address the illegal immigration problem from a unique angle. Staff members told me recently, "Mexicans don't want to cross the border. If they could stay home, they would. But they can't because they can't get jobs. So we teach them English. With English skills they can get accepted into one of Mexico's low-cost universities and find a career at home. Others see illegal immigrants; we see opportunities."

Another wall down.

We can't outlive our lives if we can't get beyond our biases. Who are your Samaritans? Ethiopian eunuchs? Whom have you been taught to distrust and avoid?

It's time to remove a few bricks.

Welcome the day God takes you to your Samaria—not so distant in miles but different in styles, tastes, tongues, and traditions.

And if you meet an Ethiopian eunuch, so different yet so sincere, don't refuse that person. Don't let class, race, gender, politics, geography, or culture hinder God's work. For the end of the matter is this: when we cross the field and cheer for the other side, everyone wins.

QUESTIONS FOR REFLECTION AND DISCUSSION

1. Philip went to Samaria, and the grace of God blasted the walls between the Jews and Samaritans. Max asks you, "Do any walls bisect your world?" What divisions do you see dominating your culture? What unspoken rules of separation promote a subconscious prejudice? How long has this wall been there? What are the root causes? What keeps it going?

2. Describe yourself with the categories Max used to describe Philip (skin, hometown, economics, relationships, etc.). Now describe someone quite the opposite of you in these categories. Name someone you know who resembles the latter.

3. As Christians, how well do we live out Galatians 3:28–29 and erase the divisions between us? Where have we succeeded? Where have we failed?

4. How could you tell a person on the other side of a dividing wall that he or she matters to you? What could you do to show that person you care?

5. Be honest with yourself about your prejudices. Spend some quiet time thinking about this. Make a list of groups of people you tend to prejudge or categorize. Pray over that piece of paper, asking God to change your heart. Then shred the list, embracing the freedom that comes with unbiased eyes.

Chapter 7

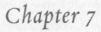

THE
PARALYZED
MAN

A few days later, when Jesus came back to Capernaum, the news spread that he was at home. Many people gathered together so that there was no room in the house, not even outside the door. And Jesus was teaching them God's message. Four people came, carrying a paralyzed man. Since they could not get to Jesus because of the crowd, they dug a hole in the roof right above where he was speaking. When they got through, they lowered the mat with the paralyzed man on it. When Jesus saw the faith of these people, he said to the paralyzed man, "Young man, your sins are forgiven."

Some of the teachers of the law were sitting there, thinking to themselves, "Why does this man say things like that? He is speaking as if he were God. Only God can forgive sins."

Jesus knew immediately what these teachers of the law were thinking. So he said to them, "Why are you thinking these things? Which is easier: to tell this paralyzed man, 'Your sins are forgiven,' or to tell him, 'Stand up. Take your mat and walk'? But I will prove to you that the Son of Man has authority on earth to forgive sins." So Jesus said to the paralyzed man, "I tell you, stand up, take your mat, and go home." Immediately the paralyzed man stood up, took his mat, and walked out while everyone was watching him.

The people were amazed and praised God. They said, "We have never seen anything like this!"

—MARK 2:1–12

THE HARDEST THING
GOD EVER DID

Let's talk for a minute about lovebursts.

You've witnessed *sunbursts*: sunlight shafting into a shadowed forest. You've seen *starbursts*: shots of light soaring through a night sky. And you've heard *powerbursts*: raw energy booming in the silence. And you've felt *lovebursts*. You may not have called them such, but you've felt them.

Lovebursts. Spontaneous affection. Tender moments of radiant love. Ignited devotion. Explosions of tenderness. May I illustrate?

You and your husband are at a party. One of those stand-in-the-living-room-and-talk-and-eat parties. You are visiting with some women, and your husband is across the room in a circle of men. The topic in your group is husbands, and the collective opinion is negative. The women complain about the amount of golf, dirty socks, and late nights at work. But you're silent. You say little because you have little to say. The guy you married isn't perfect, but he isn't a pain either. In fact, compared to these guys, he sounds pretty special. He's changed more than his share of diapers, and his golf clubs haven't come down out of the attic since the last baby was born. You look across the room at your husband and smile at the way he tugs at the tie you convinced him to wear. Still as handsome as the day you met. A bit paunchier and balder perhaps, but you don't see that. All you see is the man who stole your heart. And all of a sudden you'd go to China in a rowboat to tell him how glad you are that he did.

That's a loveburst. Here is another.

It's been awhile since you held a baby. It's been awhile since you were near a baby. But now you're alone with the baby. Your kids dropped him off at the house for the evening, and your wife ran to the store to get some milk, and now it's just you and your grandson. He's only a few days old and wrapped tighter than the cigars you gave your friends. As you cradle him in your arms, you realize this is the first time the two of you have been alone. With all the fanfare and friends at the hospital, you haven't shared a private moment—till now. So you sit in your big chair and turn him so you can see his face. You ponder the future, his future: first steps, first kiss, football, college. You wonder what it's going to be like being a kid in a world where hurt seems to linger on every corner.

As you look into the little eyes and nose that came from the other side of the family, it hits you. Out of nowhere comes a bolt of devotion. You're suddenly aware that hell itself would have to get past you to get to this one who carries your name. "It's gonna be all right," you hear yourself pledge to the sleeping boy. "Whatever happens, just remember I'm here. It's gonna be all right."

May I share one more?

You came home cranky because a deadline got moved up. She came home grumpy because the day care forgot to give your five-year-old her throat medicine. Each of you was wanting a little sympathy from the other, but neither got any. So there you sit at the dinner table—cranky and grumpy—with little Emily. Emily folds her hands to pray (as she has been taught), and the two of you bow your heads (but not your hearts) and listen. From where this prayer comes, God only knows.

"God, it's Emily. How are you? I'm fine, thank you. Mom and Dad are mad. I don't know why. We've got birds and toys and mash potatoes and each other. Maybe you can get them to stop being mad? Please do, or it's just gonna be you and me having any fun tonight. Amen."

The prayer is answered before it's finished; you both look up in the middle and laugh at the end and shake your heads and say you're sorry. And you both thank God for the little voice who reminded you about what matters.

That's what lovebursts do. They remind you about what matters. A telegram delivered to the back door of the familiar, telling you to treasure the treasure you've got while you've got it. A whisper from an angel, or someone who sounds like one, reminding you that what you have is greater than what you want and that what is urgent is not always what matters.

Those are lovebursts. You have them. I have them. And this may surprise you: Jesus had them . . . lots of them.

One of them happened when Jesus met an invalid. The man couldn't walk. He couldn't stand. His limbs were bent and his body twisted. A waist-high world walked past as he sat and watched.

Perhaps he was palsied, his body ridden with disease since birth. While other children had jumped and run, he had labored to bring a spoon to his mouth. As his brothers and sisters spoke and sang, his words slurred and slipped. Maybe he had never known what it was to be whole.

Or maybe he had known. Maybe he had once been healthy. Was there a time when he was known for his ability, not his disability? Was there an era when he could outrun anyone? Was there a time when he was the strongest in the shop? Was there a day when every kid in the village wanted to be like him?

Then came the fall—a tumble down a canyon, perhaps a stumble down some stairs. The pain in his skull was unbearable, but the numbness in his legs and arms was far worse. His feet hung like ornaments on the ends of his legs. His hands dangled like empty sleeves from his sides. He could see his limbs, but he couldn't feel them.

Whether he was born paralyzed or became paralyzed, the end result was the same: total dependence on others. Someone had to wash his face and bathe his body. He couldn't blow his nose or go on a walk. When he ran, it was in his dreams, and his dreams would always awaken to a body that couldn't roll over and couldn't go back to sleep for all the hurt the night dream had brought.

"What he needs is a new body," any man in half his mind would say. What he needs is a God in heaven to restore what tragedy has robbed: arms that swing, hands that grip, and feet that dance.

When people looked at him, they didn't see the man; they saw a body in need of a miracle. That's not what Jesus saw, but that's what the people saw. And that's certainly what his friends saw. So they did what any of us would do for a friend. They tried to get him some help.

Word was out that a carpenter-turned-teacher-turned-wonder-worker was in town. And as the word got out, the people came. They came from every hole and hovel in Israel. They came like soldiers returning from battle—bandaged, crippled, sightless. The old with prune faces and toothless mouths. The young with deaf babies and broken hearts. Fathers with sons who couldn't speak. Wives with wombs that wouldn't bear fruit. The world, it seemed, had come to see if he was real or right or both.

By the time his friends arrived at the place, the house was full. People jammed the doorways. Kids sat in the windows. Others peeked over shoulders. How would this small band of friends ever attract Jesus' attention? They had to make a choice: Do we go in or give up?

What would have happened had the friends given up? What if they had shrugged their shoulders and mumbled something about the crowd being big and dinner getting cold and turned and left? After all, they had done a good deed in coming this far. Who could fault them for turning back? You can only do so much for somebody. But these friends hadn't done enough.

One said that he had an idea. The four huddled over the paralytic and listened to the plan to climb to the top of the house, cut through the roof, and lower their friend down with their sashes.

It was risky—they could fall. It was dangerous—*he* could fall. It was unorthodox—de-roofing is antisocial. It was intrusive—Jesus was busy. But it was their only chance to see Jesus. So they climbed to the roof.

Faith does those things. Faith does the unexpected. And faith gets God's attention. Look what Mark says: "When Jesus saw the faith of these people, he said to the paralyzed man, 'Young man, your sins are forgiven'" (Mark 2:5).

Finally, someone took him at his word! Four men had enough hope in him and love for their friend that they took a chance. The stretcher above was a sign from above—somebody believes! Someone was willing to risk embarrassment and injury for just a few moments with the Galilean.

Jesus was moved.

Like the wife overwhelmed with love for her paunchy but precious husband.

Like the grandfather determined to protect his grandson.

Like the parents touched by the prayer of their child.

Jesus was moved by the scene of faith. So he applauds—if not with his hands, at least with his heart. And not only does he applaud, he blesses. And we witness a divine loveburst.

The friends want him to heal their friend. But Jesus won't settle for a simple healing of the body—he wants to heal the soul. He leapfrogs the physical and deals with the spiritual. To heal the body is temporal; to heal the soul is eternal.

The request of the friends is valid—but timid. The expectations of the crowd are high—but not high enough. They expect Jesus to say, "I heal you." Instead he says, "I forgive you."

They expect him to treat the body, for that is what they see.

He chooses to treat not only the body, but also the spiritual, for that is what he sees.

They want Jesus to give the man a new body so he can walk. Jesus gives grace so the man can live.

Remarkable. Sometimes God is so touched by what he sees that he gives us what we need and not simply that for which we ask.

It's a good thing. For who would have ever thought to ask God for what he gives? Which of us would have dared to say: "God, would you please hang yourself on a tool of torture as a substitution for every mistake I have ever committed?" And then have the audacity to add: "And after you forgive me, could you prepare me a place in your house to live forever?"

And if that wasn't enough: "And would you please live within me and protect me and guide me and bless me with more than I could ever deserve?"

Honestly, would we have the chutzpah to ask for that? No, we, like the friends, would have only asked for the small stuff.

We would ask for little things like a long life and a healthy body and a good job. Grand requests from our perspective, but from God's it's like taking the moped when he offers the limo.

So, knowing the paralytic didn't know enough to ask for what he needed, Jesus gave it anyway: "Young man, your sins are forgiven" (v. 5).

The Pharisees start to grumble. That's not kosher. Even a tenderfoot Jew knows, "Only God can forgive sins" (v. 7).

Their mumbling spawns one of Christ's greatest questions: "Which is easier: to tell this paralyzed man, 'Your sins are forgiven,' or to tell him, 'Stand up. Take your mat and walk'?" (v. 9).

You answer the question. Which is easier for Jesus? To forgive a soul or heal a body? Which caused Jesus less pain—providing this man with health or providing this man with heaven?

To heal the man's body took a simple command; to forgive the man's sins took Jesus' blood. The first was done in the house of friends; the second on a hill with thieves. One took a word; the other took his body. One took a moment; the other took his life.

Which was easier?

So strong was his love for this crew of faith that he went beyond their appeal and went straight to the cross.

Jesus already knows the cost of grace. He already knows the price of forgiveness. But he offers it anyway. Love burst his heart.

By the way, he hasn't changed. What happened then happens today. When we take a step of faith, God sees. The same face that beamed at the paralytic beams at the alcoholic refusing the bottle. The same eyes that danced at the friends dance at the mom and dad who will do whatever it takes to get their child to Jesus. And the same lips that spoke to the man in Capernaum speak to the man in Detroit, to the woman in

Belfast, to the child in Moscow . . . to any person anywhere who dares to come into the presence of God and ask for help.

And though we can't hear it here, the angels can hear him there. All of heaven must pause as another burst of love declares the only words that really matter: "Your sins are forgiven."

QUESTIONS FOR REFLECTION AND DISCUSSION

1. Max writes that lovebursts remind you "that what you have is greater than what you want and that what is urgent is not always what matters." How do lovebursts do this? Name a few examples from your own life where you have seen this principle at work.

2. Had the paralyzed man's friends given up when they saw the full house, what do you suppose would have happened to the man? Do you have any friends who would go as far to help you as this man's friends did for him? Are you such a friend for anyone else?

3. Max writes, "Faith does the unexpected. And faith gets God's attention." While acting in faith, have you ever done the unexpected? If so, what happened?

4. Comment on the following statement: "They want Jesus to give the man a new body so he can walk. Jesus gives grace so the man can live." What implications does this have for our day-to-day lives?

5. Are you glad that God often bypasses our requests and gives us what we need instead? Explain.

Chapter 8

❦

NOAH

After forty days Noah opened the window he had made in the ark and sent out a raven, and it kept flying back and forth until the water had dried up from the earth. Then he sent out a dove to see if the water had receded from the surface of the ground. But the dove could find no place to set its feet because there was water over all the surface of the earth; so it returned to Noah in the ark. He reached out his hand and took the dove and brought it back to himself in the ark. He waited seven more days and again sent out the dove from the ark. When the dove returned to him in the evening, there in its beak was a freshly plucked olive leaf! Then Noah knew that the water had receded from the earth.

—GENESIS 8:6–11 NIV

When You're Low on Hope

Water. All Noah can see is water. The evening sun sinks into it. The clouds are reflected in it. His boat is surrounded by it. Water. Water to the north. Water to the south. Water to the east. Water to the west. Water.

All Noah can see is water.

He can't remember when he's seen anything but. He and the boys had barely pushed the last hippo up the ramp when heaven opened a thousand fire hydrants. Within moments the boat was rocking, and for days the rain was pouring, and for weeks Noah has been wondering, *How long is this going to last?* For forty days it rained. For months they have floated. For months they have eaten the same food, smelled the same smell, and looked at the same faces. After a certain point you run out of things to say to each other.

Finally the boat bumped, and the rocking stopped. Mrs. Noah gave Mr. Noah a look, and Noah gave the hatch a shove and poked his head through. The hull of the ark was resting on ground, but the ground was still surrounded by water. "Noah," she yelled up at him, "what do you see?"

"Water."

He sent a raven on a scouting mission; it never returned. He sent a dove. It came back shivering and spent, having found no place to roost. Then, just this morning, he tried again. He pulled a dove out of the bowels of the ark and ascended the ladder. The morning sun caused them both to squint. As he kissed the breast of the bird, he felt a pounding heart. Had he put a hand on his chest, he would have felt another. With a prayer he let it go and watched until the bird was no bigger than a speck on a window.

All day he looked for the dove's return. In between chores he opened the hatch and searched. The boys wanted him to play a little pin the tail on the donkey, but he passed. He chose instead to climb into the crow's nest and look. The wind lifted his gray hair. The sun warmed his weather-beaten face. But nothing lifted his heavy heart. He had seen nothing. Not in the morning. Not after lunch. Not later.

Now the sun is setting, and the sky is darkening, and he has come to look one final time, but all he sees is water. Water to the north. Water to the south. Water to the east. Water to the . . .

You know the feeling. You have stood where Noah stood. You've known your share of floods. Flooded by sorrow at the cemetery, stress at the office, anger at the disability in your body or the inability of your spouse. You've seen the floodwater rise, and you've likely seen the sun set on your hopes as well. You've been on Noah's boat.

And you've needed what Noah needed; you've needed some hope. You're not asking for a helicopter rescue, but the sound of one would be nice. Hope doesn't promise an instant solution but rather the possibility of an eventual one. Sometimes all we need is a little hope.

That's all Noah needed. And that's all Noah received.

The old sailor stares at the sun bisected by the horizon. Could hardly imagine a more beautiful sight. But he'd give this one and a hundred more for an acre of dry ground and a grove of grapes. Mrs. Noah's voice reminds him that dinner is on the table and he should lock the hatch, and he's just about to call it a day when he hears the cooing of the dove. Here is how the Bible describes the moment: "When the dove returned to him in the evening, there in its beak was a freshly plucked olive leaf!" (Gen. 8:11 NIV).

An olive leaf. Noah would have been happy to have the bird but to have the leaf! This leaf was more than foliage; this was promise. The bird brought more than a piece of a tree; it brought hope. For isn't that what hope is? Hope is an olive leaf—evidence of dry land after a flood. Proof to the dreamer that dreaming is worth the risk.

Don't we love the olive leaves of life?

"It appears the cancer may be in remission."

"I can help you with those finances."

"We'll get through this together."

What's more, don't we love the doves that bring them? When the father walks his son through his first broken heart, he gives him an olive leaf. When the wife of many years consoles the wife of a few months, when she tells her that conflicts come and all husbands are moody and these storms pass, you know what she is doing? She is giving an olive leaf.

We love olive leaves. And we love those who give them.

Perhaps that's the reason so many loved Jesus.

He stands near a woman who was yanked from a bed of promiscuity. She's still dizzy from the raid. A door slammed open, covers were pulled back, and the fraternity of moral police barged in. And now here she stands. Noah could see nothing but water. She can see nothing but anger. She has no hope.

But then Jesus speaks, "If any one of you is without sin, let him be the first to throw a stone at her" (John 8:7 NIV). Silence. Both the eyes and the rocks of the accusers hit the ground. Within moments they have left, and Jesus is alone with the woman. The dove of heaven offers her a leaf.

"Woman, where are they? Has no one condemned you?"

"No one, sir," she said.

"Then neither do I condemn you," Jesus declared. "Go now and leave your life of sin." (vv. 10–11 NIV)

Into her shame-flooded world he brings a leaf of hope.

He does something similar for Martha. She is bobbing in a sea of sorrow. Her brother is dead. His body has been buried. And Jesus, well, Jesus is late. "If you had been here, my brother would not have died." Then I think she might have paused. "But I know that even now God will give you whatever you ask" (John 11:21–22 NIV). As Noah opened his hatch, so Martha opens her heart. As the dove brought a leaf, so Christ brings the same.

> "I am the resurrection and the life. He who believes in me will live, even though he dies; and whoever lives and believes in me will never die. Do you believe this?"
>
> "Yes, Lord," she told him, "I believe that you are the Christ, the Son of God, who was to come into the world." (vv. 25–27 NIV)

How could he get by with such words? Who was he to make such a claim? What qualified him to offer grace to one woman and a promise of resurrection to another? Simple. He had done what the dove did. He'd crossed the shoreline of the future land and journeyed among the trees. And from the grove of grace he plucked a leaf for the woman. And from the tree of life he pulled a sprig for Martha.

And from both he brings leaves to you. Grace and life. Forgiveness of sin. The defeat of death. This is the hope he gives. This is the hope we need.

In his book *The Grand Essentials*, Ben Patterson tells of an S-4 submarine that sank off the coast of Massachusetts. The entire crew was trapped. Every effort was made to rescue the sailors, but every effort failed. Near the end of the ordeal, a deep-sea diver heard tapping on the steel wall of the sunken sub. As he placed his helmet against the vessel, he realized he was hearing a sailor tap out this question in Morse code: "Is there any hope?"[1]

To the guilty who ask that question, Jesus says, "Yes!"

To the death-struck who ask that question, Jesus answers, "Yes!"

To all the Noahs of the world, to all who search the horizon for a fleck of hope, he proclaims, "Yes!" And he comes. He comes as a dove. He comes bearing fruit from a distant land, from our future home. He comes with a leaf of hope.

Have you received yours? Don't think your ark is too isolated. Don't think your flood is too wide. Your toughest challenge is nothing more than bobby pins and rubber bands to God. *Bobby pins and rubber bands?*

My older sister used to give them to me when I was a child. I would ride my tricycle up and down the sidewalk, pretending that the bobby pins were keys and my trike was a truck. But one day I lost the "keys." Crisis! What was I going to do? My search yielded nothing but tears and fear. But when I confessed my mistake to my sister, she just smiled. Being a decade older, she had a better perspective.

God has a better perspective as well. With all due respect, our severest struggles are, in his view, nothing worse than lost bobby pins and rubber bands. He is not confounded, confused, or discouraged.

Receive his hope, won't you? Receive it because you need it. Receive it so you can share it.

What do you suppose Noah did with his? What do you think he did with the leaf? Did he throw it overboard and forget about it? Do you suppose he stuck it in his pocket and saved it for a scrapbook? Or do you think he let out a whoop and assembled the troops and passed it around like the Hope Diamond it was?

Certainly he whooped. That's what you do with hope. What do you do with olive leaves? You pass them around. You don't stick them in your pocket. You give them to the ones you love. Love always hopes. "Love . . . bears all things, believes all things, *hopes* all things, endures all things" (1 Cor. 13:4–7 NKJV; emphasis added).

Love has hope in you.

The aspiring young author was in need of hope. More than one person had told him to give up. "Getting published is impossible," one mentor said. "Unless you are a national celebrity, publishers won't talk to you." Another warned, "Writing takes too much time. Besides, you don't want all your thoughts on paper."

Initially he listened. He agreed that writing was a waste of effort and turned his attention to other projects. But somehow the pen and pad were bourbon and Coke to the wordaholic. He'd rather write than read. So he wrote. How many nights did he pass on that couch in the corner of the apartment reshuffling his deck of verbs and nouns? And how many hours did his wife sit with him? He wordsmithing. She cross-stitching. Finally a manuscript was finished. Crude and laden with mistakes but finished.

She gave him the shove. "Send it out. What's the harm?"

So out it went. Mailed to fifteen different publishers. While the couple waited, he wrote. While he wrote, she stitched. Neither expecting much, both hoping everything. Responses began to fill the mailbox. "I'm sorry, but we don't accept unsolicited manuscripts." "We must return your work. Best of luck." "Our catalog doesn't have room for unpublished authors."

I still have those letters. Somewhere in a file. Finding them would take some time. Finding Denalyn's cross-stitch, however, would take none. To see it, all I do is lift my eyes from this monitor and look on the wall. "Of all those arts in which the wise excel, nature's chief master-piece is writing well."

She gave it to me about the time the fifteenth letter arrived. A publisher had said yes. That letter is also framed. Which of the two is more meaningful? The gift from my wife or the letter from the publisher? The gift, hands down. For in giving the gift, Denalyn gave hope.

Love does that. Love extends an olive leaf to the loved one and says, "I have hope in you."

Love is just as quick to say, "I have hope *for* you."

You can say those words. You are a flood survivor. By God's grace you have found your way to dry land. You know what it's like to see the waters subside. And since you do, since you passed through a flood and lived to tell about it, you are qualified to give hope to someone else.

What? Can't think of any floods in your past? Let me jog your memory.

How about adolescence? Remember the torrent of the teenage years? Remember the hormones and hemlines? The puberty and pimples? Those were tough times. *Yeah*, you're thinking, *but you get through them*. That's exactly what teenagers need to hear you say. They need an olive leaf from a survivor.

So do young couples. It happens in every marriage. The honeymoon ends, and the river of romance becomes the river of reality, and they wonder if they will survive. You can tell them they will. You've been through it. Wasn't easy, but you survived. You and your spouse found dry land. Why don't you pluck an olive leaf and take it to an ark?

Are you a cancer survivor? Someone in the cancer ward needs to hear from you. Have you buried a spouse and lived to smile again? Then find the recently widowed and walk with them. Your experiences have deputized you into the dove brigade. You have an opportunity—yea, verily an obligation—to give hope to the arkbound.

Remember Paul's admonition?

> What a wonderful God we have—he is the Father of our Lord Jesus Christ, the source of every mercy, and the one who so wonderfully comforts and strengthens us in our hardships and trials. And why does he do this? So that when others are troubled, needing our sympathy and encouragement, we can pass on to them this same help and comfort God has given us. (2 Cor. 1:3–4 TLB)

Encourage those who are struggling. Don't know what to say? Then open your Bible. The olive leaf for the Christian is a verse of Scripture. "For everything that was written in the past was written to teach us, so that through endurance and the encouragement of the Scriptures we might have hope" (Rom. 15:4 NIV).

Do you have a Bible? Do you know a Noah? Then start passing out the leaves.

To the grief stricken: "God has said, 'Never will I leave you; never will I forsake you'" (Heb. 13:5 NIV).

To the guilt ridden: "There is now no condemnation for those who are in Christ Jesus" (Rom. 8:1 NIV).

To the jobless: "In all things God works for the good of those who love him" (Rom. 8:28 NIV).

To those who feel beyond God's grace: "Whoever believes in him shall not perish but have eternal life" (John 3:16 NIV).

Your Bible is a basket of leaves. Won't you share one? They have amazing impact. After receiving his, Noah was a changed man. "Then Noah knew that the water had receded from the earth" (Gen. 8:11 NIV). He went up the ladder with questions and came down the ladder with confidence.

What a difference one leaf makes.

Questions for Reflection and Discussion

1. In what areas of your life do you need hope right now? How has hope rescued you from a "flood" in the past?

2. "Hope doesn't promise an instant solution but rather the possibility of an eventual one. Sometimes all we need is a little hope." Who do you know who could use a little hope right now?

3. In what ways can you "pass out an olive leaf" to your loved ones? If you told them you have hope in them and for them, what would that mean to them?

4. Why did Paul not grumble about his present struggles (Rom. 8:18)?

5. How can Paul's understanding of hope (Rom. 8:24–25) help us in our difficult times?

Chapter 9

❦

THE WOMAN CAUGHT IN ADULTERY

Jesus went to the Mount of Olives. But early in the morning he went back to the Temple, and all the people came to him, and he sat and taught them. The teachers of the law and the Pharisees brought a woman who had been caught in adultery. They forced her to stand before the people. They said to Jesus, "Teacher, this woman was caught having sexual relations with a man who is not her husband. The law of Moses commands that we stone to death every woman who does this. What do you say we should do?" They were asking this to trick Jesus so that they could have some charge against him.

But Jesus bent over and started writing on the ground with his finger. When they continued to ask Jesus their question, he raised up and said, "Anyone here who has never sinned can throw the first stone at her." Then Jesus bent over again and wrote on the ground.

Those who heard Jesus began to leave one by one, first the older men and then the others. Jesus was left there alone with the woman standing before him. Jesus raised up again and asked her, "Woman, where are they? Has no one judged you guilty?"

She answered, "No one, sir."

Then Jesus said, "I also don't judge you guilty. You may go now, but don't sin anymore."

—JOHN 8:1–11

OVERCOMING SHAME

Rebecca Thompson fell twice from the Fremont Canyon Bridge. She died both times. The first fall broke her heart; the second broke her neck.

She was only eighteen years of age when she and her eleven-year-old sister were abducted by a pair of hoodlums near a store in Casper, Wyoming. They drove the girls forty miles southwest to the Fremont Canyon Bridge, a one-lane, steel-beamed structure rising 112 feet above the North Platte River.

The men brutally beat and raped Rebecca. She somehow convinced them not to do the same to her sister Amy. Both were thrown over the bridge into the narrow gorge. Amy died when she landed on a rock near the river, but Rebecca slammed into a ledge and was ricocheted into deeper water.

With a hip fractured in five places, she struggled to the shore. To protect her body from the cold, she wedged herself between two rocks and waited until the dawn.

But the dawn never came for Rebecca. Oh, the sun came up, and she was found. The physicians treated her wounds, and the courts imprisoned her attackers. Life continued, but the dawn never came.

The blackness of her night of horrors lingered. She was never able to climb out of the canyon. So in September 1992, nineteen years later, she returned to the bridge.

Against her boyfriend's pleadings, she drove seventy miles per hour to the North Platte River. With her two-year-old daughter and boyfriend at her side, she sat on the edge of the Fremont Canyon Bridge and wept. Through her tears she retold the story. The boyfriend didn't want the child to see her mother cry, so he carried the toddler to the car.

That's when he heard her body hit the water.

And that's when Rebecca Thompson died her second death. The sun never dawned on Rebecca's dark night. Why? What eclipsed the light from her world?

Fear? Perhaps. She had testified against the men, pointing them out in the courtroom. One of the murderers had taunted her by smirking and sliding his finger across his throat. On the day of her death, the two had been up for parole. Perhaps the fear of a second encounter was too great.

Was it anger? Anger at her rapists? Anger at the parole board? Anger at herself for the thousand falls in the thousand nightmares that followed? Or anger at God for a canyon that grew ever deeper and a night that grew ever blacker and a dawn that never came?

Was it guilt? Some think so. Despite Rebecca's attractive smile and appealing personality, friends say that she struggled with the ugly fact that she had survived and her little sister had not.

Was it shame? Everyone she knew and thousands she didn't had heard the humiliating details of her tragedy. The stigma was tattooed deeper with the newspaper ink of every headline. She had been raped. She had been violated. She had been shamed. And try as she might to outlive and outrun the memory . . . she never could.

So nineteen years later she went back to the bridge.

Canyons of shame run deep. Gorges of never-ending guilt. Walls ribboned with the greens and grays of death. Unending echoes of screams. Put your hands over your ears. Splash water on your face. Stop looking over your shoulder. Try as you might to outrun yesterday's tragedies— their tentacles are longer than your hope. They draw you back to the bridge of sorrows to be shamed again and again and again.

If it were your fault, it would be different. If you were to blame, you could apologize. If the tumble into the canyon were your mistake, you could respond. But you weren't a volunteer. You were a victim.

Sometimes your shame is private. Pushed over the edge by an abusive spouse. Molested by a perverted parent. Seduced by a compromising superior. No one else knows. But you know. And that's enough.

Sometimes it's public. Branded by a divorce you didn't want. Contaminated by a disease you never expected. Marked by a handicap you didn't create. And whether it's actually in their eyes or just in your imagination, you have to deal with it—you are marked: a divorcée, an invalid, an orphan, an AIDS patient.

Whether private or public, shame is always painful. And unless you deal with it, it is permanent. Unless you get help—the dawn will never come.

You're not surprised when I say there are Rebecca Thompsons in every city and Fremont Bridges in every town. And there are many Rebecca Thompsons in the Bible. So many, in fact, that it almost seems that the pages of Scripture are stitched together with their stories. You've met many in this book. Each acquainted with the hard floor of the canyon of shame.

But there is one woman whose story embodies them all. A story of failure. A story of abuse. A story of shame.

And a story of grace.

That's her, the woman standing in the center of the circle. Those men around her are religious leaders. Pharisees, they are called. Self-appointed custodians of conduct. And the other man, the one in the simple clothes, the one sitting on the ground, the one looking at the face of the woman, that's Jesus.

Jesus has been teaching.

The woman has been cheating.

And the Pharisees are out to stop them both.

"Teacher, this woman was caught in the act of adultery" (John 8:4 NIV). The accusation rings off the courtyard walls.

"Caught in the act of adultery." The words alone are enough to make you blush. Doors slammed open. Covers jerked back.

"In the act." In the arms. In the moment. In the embrace.

"Caught." Aha! What have we here? This man is not your husband. Put on some clothes! We know what to do with women like you!

In an instant she is yanked from private passion to public spectacle.

Heads poke out of windows as the posse pushes her through the streets. Dogs bark. Neighbors turn. The city sees. Clutching a thin robe around her shoulders, she hides her nakedness.

But nothing can hide her shame.

From this second on, she'll be known as an adulteress. When she goes to the market, women will whisper. When she passes, heads will turn. When her name is mentioned, the people will remember.

Moral failure finds easy recall.

The greater travesty, however, goes unnoticed. What the woman did is shameful, but what the Pharisees did is despicable. According to the law, adultery was punishable by death, but only if two people witnessed the act. There had to be two eyewitnesses.

Question: How likely are two people to be eyewitnesses to adultery? What are the chances of two people stumbling upon an early morning flurry of forbidden embraces? Unlikely. But if you do, odds are it's not a coincidence.

So we wonder. How long did the men peer through the window before they barged in? How long did they lurk behind the curtain before they stepped out?

And what of the man? Adultery requires two participants. What happened to him? Could it be that he slipped out?

The evidence leaves little doubt. It was a trap. She's been caught. But she'll soon see that she is not the catch—she's only the bait.

"The law of Moses commands that we stone to death every woman who does this. What do you say we should do?" (v. 5).

Pretty cocky, this committee of high ethics. Pretty proud of themselves, these agents of righteousness. This will be a moment they long remember, the morning they foil and snag the mighty Nazarene.

As for the woman? Why, she's immaterial. Merely a pawn in their game. Her future? It's unimportant. Her reputation? Who cares if it's ruined? She is a necessary, yet dispensable, part of their plan.

The woman stares at the ground. Her sweaty hair dangles. Her tears drip hot with hurt. Her lips are tight; her jaw is clenched. She knows she's been framed. No need to look up. She'll find no kindness. She looks at the stones in their hands. Squeezed so tightly that fingertips turn white.

She thinks of running. But where? She could claim mistreatment. But to whom? She could deny the act, but she was seen. She could beg for mercy, but these men offer none.

The woman has nowhere to turn.

You'd expect Jesus to stand and proclaim judgment on the hypocrites. He doesn't. You'd hope that he would snatch the woman and the two would be beamed to Galilee. That's not what happens either. You'd imagine that an angel would descend or heaven would speak or the earth would shake. No, none of that.

Once again, his move is subtle.

But, once again, his message is unmistakable.

What does Jesus do? (If you already know, pretend you don't and feel the surprise.)

Jesus writes in the sand.

He stoops down and draws in the dirt. The same finger that engraved the commandments on Sinai's peak and seared the warning on Belshazzar's wall now scribbles on the courtyard floor. And as he writes, he speaks: "Anyone here who has never sinned can throw the first stone at her" (v. 7).

The young look to the old. The old look in their hearts. They are the first to drop their stones. And as they turn to leave, the young who were cocky with borrowed convictions do the same. The only sound is the thud of rocks and the shuffle of feet.

Jesus and the woman are left alone. With the jury gone, the courtroom becomes the judge's chambers, and the woman awaits his verdict. *Surely, a sermon is brewing. No doubt, he's going to demand that I apologize.* But the judge doesn't speak. His head is down; perhaps he's still writing in the sand. He seems surprised when he realizes that she is still there.

"Woman, where are they? Has no one judged you guilty?"

She answers, "No one, sir."

Then Jesus says, "I also don't judge you guilty. You may go now, but don't sin anymore" (vv. 10–11).

If you have ever wondered how God reacts when you fail, frame these words and hang them on the wall. Read them. Ponder them. Drink from them. Stand below them and let them wash over your soul.

Or better still, take him with you to your canyon of shame. Invite Christ to journey with you back to the Fremont Bridge of your world. Let him stand beside you as you retell the events of the darkest nights of your soul.

And then listen. Listen carefully. He's speaking.

"I don't judge you guilty."

And watch. Watch carefully. He's writing. He's leaving a message. Not in the sand, but on a cross.

Not with his hand, but with his blood.

His message has two words: not guilty.

QUESTIONS FOR REFLECTION AND DISCUSSION

1. Max writes, "Whether private or public, shame is always painful. And unless you deal with it, it is permanent. Unless you get help—the dawn will never come." What do you think he means? Do you agree with him? Why or why not?

2. What does the word *shame* mean to you? What does the word *grace* mean to you? Which is the stronger term? Why?

3. With what character in the story of John 8 do you identify most closely? The woman? The guilty (but absent) man? The Pharisees? The men in the crowd? Explain your choice.

4. Jesus told the woman, "I also don't judge you guilty. You may go now, but don't sin anymore" (John 8:11). Does any part of this statement bother you? Is it what you would have expected Jesus to say? Why?

5. Do the words "not guilty" apply to you? Explain your answer. How do those words make you feel?

Chapter 10

PETER AND JOHN

The priests, the captain of the temple, and the Sadducees came upon them.

—ACTS 4:1 NKJV

WHEN PERSECUTION COMES

On April 18, 2007, three Christians in Turkey were killed for their beliefs. Necati Aydin was one of them. He was a thirty-five-year-old pastor in the city of Malatya.

He nearly didn't go to his office that morning. He'd been traveling for ten days and his wife, Semse, wanted him to stay home and rest. She fed breakfast to their two children, Elisha and Esther, and took them to school. Upon returning, she walked softly so as not to awaken her husband. Even so, he stirred, squinted, opened his arms, and admitted his weariness. "I don't want to get up today."

But he did. There was much work to do. Only 0.2 percent of the mainly Muslim nation follows Jesus. Ironic. The land once knew the sandal prints of the apostle Paul and provided a stage for the first churches. But today? Turkish Christ worshippers number less than 153,000 in a nation of 76 million.[1] People such as Necati live to change that. He pulled his weary body out of bed and got ready for the day.

As Semse remembers and retells the events of that morning, she pauses between sentences. Her round cheeks flush with pink. Dark hair sweeps in a wave across her forehead. Until this point she's been able to contain the emotion. She described the attack, the cruelty, and the harshness of sudden widowhood without tears. But at this sentence, they press through. "My dear husband walked out the door at eleven. I was waiting for him to get on the elevator. There he smiled at me one last time, but I didn't know that was the last smile. That's what I'll always remember . . ."

She sighs and looks away as if seeing a face only she can see. Then back. "This is a painful thing for me because I miss his smile . . . because the sun doesn't rise when he doesn't smile . . ."

Semse looks down and permits a soft sob, but only one. "It's a bitter cup, and we have to drink of it every day."

By the time Necati reached the office, his two colleagues had already received visitors: five young men who had expressed an interest in the Christian faith. But the inquisitors brought more than questions. They brought guns, bread knives, ropes, and towels.

The attackers brandished their weapons and told Necati to pray the Islamic prayer of conversion: "There is no God except Allah, and Muhammad is his prophet."

When Necati refused, the torture began. For an agonizing hour the assailants bound, interrogated, and cut the Christians. Finally, with the police pounding on the door, they sliced the throats of the victims. The last word heard from the office was the cry of an unswerving Christian: "Messiah! Messiah!"[2]

Such stories have a way of silencing us. This morning's traffic jam is no longer worth the mention. While I might see myself—for a microsecond—as a man of faith, I ponder the martyrs of Malatya and wonder, *Would I make the sacrifice? Would I cry out, "Messiah! Messiah!"? Would I give up my life?* Why, some days I don't want to give up my parking spot.

The Turkish pastors could have lived. With their simple confession of Allah, knives would have been lowered and lives spared. Semse would have her husband, and Elisha and Esther would have their father. Necati could have gone home to his family. He chose, instead, to speak up for Christ.

What would you have done?

The question is more than academic. Persecution comes. Three-fourths of Christians live in the third world, often in anti-Christian environments. More Chinese take part in Sunday worship than the entirety of western Europeans. Lebanon is 39 percent Christian; Sudan, 5 percent; Egypt, about 10 percent.[3] Many of these saints worship at their own risk. You may be one of them. You may be the only Christian in your Iraqi university. You may be an Arab woman who offers prayers in silence or a Messianic Jew who lives in the heart of Jerusalem.

Or perhaps you indwell a society of religious freedom but a community of spiritual oppression. You may not face blades and terrorists but critics and accusers. Family members mock your beliefs. University professors belittle your convictions. Classmates snicker at your choices. Colleagues pressure you to compromise your integrity. Coworkers make it their mission to snag you in a weak moment. Knife to your neck? No. But pressure to abandon your convictions?

I'm thinking of Maria Dutton, my Portuguese teacher when I was a missionary in Brazil. She grew up in an aristocratic and influential family. When she became a Christian, her father disowned her. He didn't attend her wedding or see her at holidays. For several years he had nothing to do with her or her children.

Heidi is the only believer on the high school cheerleading squad. When the others go wild after games, she goes home. When they party on road trips, she goes to the hotel. She is the piñata for their ridicule.

Persecution happens. Peter and John can tell you. They healed the cripple one minute and faced harassment the next. "Now as they [Peter and John] spoke to the people, the priests, the captain of the temple, and the Sadducees came upon them, being greatly disturbed that they taught the people and preached in Jesus the resurrection from the dead" (Acts 4:1–2 NKJV).

Thus far the early church had enjoyed smooth sailing. The Pentecost miracle harvested three thousand followers. The church gave birth to acts of kindness, compassion, and fellowship. Their good deeds authenticated their good news. The number of followers grew. The first three chapters of Acts are happy days. But then comes Acts 4. The church is barely out of the maternity ward, and in walk the town bullies: "the priests, the captain of the temple, and the Sadducees came upon them" (v. 1 NKJV).

A brawny soldier presses through the crowd. He wears heavy ringlets of shoulder-length hair. His naked chest bulges, and his massive legs seem to be poured iron. A medallion of authority hangs on his chest, and he carries a whip in his hand. He can, by law, arrest anyone who transgresses the temple courts. He has come to enforce the law.

The priests follow him: Caiaphas and his father-in-law, Annas. They stand on either side of the temple captain and cross their arms and glare this implicit warning: "Don't forget what we did to your Messiah. Didn't the three spikes on the Roman cross make it clear?"

Annas, the high priest, arches an eyebrow in the direction of Peter. He has not forgotten what this apostle did to his servant a few weeks ago in the Garden of Gethsemane. When the servant and the soldiers came to arrest Jesus, Peter drew his sword and "struck the high priest's servant, and cut off his right ear" (John 18:10 NKJV). Jesus healed the ear, but the high priest has not forgotten the incident. I'm envisioning Annas tugging his ear and menacing, "I have a score to settle with you, Peter."

Peter, meanwhile, may be wrestling with a few Thursday night memories of his own. Not just about his slashing sword, but also his dashing feet. He and the other followers scooted out of the garden like scalded puppies, leaving Jesus to face his foes all alone. Later that night Peter mustered up enough loyalty to appear at Jesus' trial. But when people recognized him, Peter wilted again. He denied his Savior, not once, but three times.

So far the score is Persecution–2, Peter–0. Peter has failed every test of persecution. But he won't fail this one.

The trio stands firm. If their legs tremble, it's because the beggar just learned to stand and the apostles are choosing not to run.

> Peter, filled with the Holy Spirit, said to them, "Rulers of the people and elders of Israel: If we this day are judged for a good deed done to a helpless man, by what means he has been made well, let it be known to you all, and to all the people of Israel, that by the name of Jesus Christ of Nazareth, whom you crucified, whom God raised from the dead, by Him this man stands here before you whole." (Acts 4:8–10 NKJV)

No back down in those words. I detect a touch of cynicism ("If we this day are judged for a good deed done to a helpless man . . .") and a large dose of declaration ("let it be known to you all, and to all the people of Israel, that by the name of Jesus Christ of Nazareth . . ."). Just the name Jesus would have sufficed, but Peter unapologetically replies, "Jesus Christ of Nazareth." And then he states clearly, potently, and firmly, "There is no other name under heaven given among men by which we must be saved" (v. 12 NKJV).

Annas and Caiaphas snarl their lips. The temple captain squeezes his whip. The eyes of the Sadducees narrow into tiny slits. The power brokers of Jerusalem glare at Peter and John.

But they don't budge an inch. What has happened to them? The last time they saw these soldiers, Peter and John left them in their rear-view mirror. But today they go chin to chin with the Supreme Court of Jerusalem. What's gotten into them?

Luke gives us the answer in verse 13: "Now when [the accusers] saw the boldness of Peter and John, and perceived that they were uneducated and untrained men, they marveled. And they realized that they had been with Jesus" (NKJV).

Peter and John had been with Jesus. The resurrected Jesus. In the Upper Room when he walked through the wall. Standing next to Thomas when the disciple touched the wounds. On the beach when Jesus cooked the fish. Sitting at Jesus' feet for forty days as he explained the ways of the kingdom.

They had lingered long and delightfully in the presence of the resurrected King. Awakening with him, walking with him. And because they had, silence was no longer an option. "We cannot but speak the things which we have seen and heard" (v. 20 NKJV).

Could you use some high-octane boldness? If you want to outlive your life, you could. As long as you are stationary, no one will complain. Dogs don't bark at parked cars. But as soon as you accelerate—once you step out of drunkenness into sobriety, dishonesty into integrity, or lethargy into compassion—expect the yapping to begin. Expect to be criticized. Expect to be mocked. Expect to be persecuted.

So how can we prepare ourselves? Simple. Imitate the disciples. Linger long and often in the presence of Christ. Meditate on his grace.

Ponder his love. Memorize his words. Gaze into his face. Talk to him. Courage comes as we live with Jesus.

Peter said it this way. "Don't give the opposition a second thought. Through thick and thin, keep your hearts at attention, in adoration before Christ, your Master. Be ready to speak up and tell anyone who asks why you're living the way you are, and always with the utmost courtesy" (1 Peter 3:14–15 MSG).

As we meditate on Christ's life, we find strength for our own. The example of Xu Yonghai comes to mind. A Christian in Communist China, he worked to see the legalization of house churches. The government responded by locking him in a Beijing prison for twenty-four months. His cell was eight feet by eight feet. There was no bathroom, only a pipe in a corner from which water flowed onto the concrete.

"My cell was the last stop for prisoners sentenced to die," he said. "At times there were as many as three other prisoners in the tiny, damp room, awaiting their date with the executioner."

Yonghai survived through prayer, meditation, and writing. On the walls of his cell, he wrote the major points for a book about God, using a bar of soap. Once he finished, he committed the thoughts to memory. Upon his release he turned his prison thoughts into a fifty-thousand-word book entitled *God the Creator*. Like Peter and John, Yonghai tarried in the presence of Jesus and found strength. Courage comes as we ponder the accomplishments of Christ.[4]

Would you be bold tomorrow? Then be with Jesus today. Be in his Word. Be with his people. Be in his presence. And when persecution comes (and it will), be strong. Who knows? People may realize that you, like the disciples, have been with Christ.

Questions for Reflection and Discussion

1. How do you feel when you hear stories about heroic martyrs such as Necati or stories about horrible persecution around the world? In what ways does it put your own difficulties into perspective?

2. In societies with religious freedom, we may not experience persecution, but we may experience spiritual opposition from critics, accusers, family members, professors, classmates, coworkers, and others in our daily lives. As you read that list, does it remind you of a situation that led you to silence your beliefs?

3. How do you think Peter felt in John 18:15–18, 25–27? Have you ever failed to speak out in the face of pressure or persecution? On the other hand, when have you been like Peter before his accusers in Acts 4:5–13—ready to speak the truth boldly in the face of pressure or persecution?

4. What habits have you developed in order to spend time with Jesus so you can linger long and often in his presence? How could such habits help others realize you have been with him?

5. In what ways should spiritual disciplines develop boldness in a believer?

Chapter 11

❦

NICODEMUS

There was a man named Nicodemus who was one of the Pharisees and an important Jewish leader. One night Nicodemus came to Jesus and said, "Teacher, we know you are a teacher sent from God, because no one can do the miracles you do unless God is with him."

Jesus answered, "I tell you the truth, unless you are born again, you cannot be in God's kingdom."

Nicodemus said, "But if a person is already old, how can he be born again? He cannot enter his mother's womb again. So how can a person be born a second time?"

But Jesus answered, "I tell you the truth, unless you are born from water and the Spirit, you cannot enter God's kingdom. Human life comes from human parents, but spiritual life comes from the Spirit. Don't be surprised when I tell you, 'You must all be born again.' The wind blows where it wants to and you hear the sound of it, but you don't know where the wind comes from or where it is going. It is the same with every person who is born from the Spirit."

Nicodemus asked, "How can this happen?"

Jesus said, "You are an important teacher in Israel, and you don't understand these things? I tell you the truth, we talk about what we know, and we tell about what we have seen, but you don't accept what we tell you. I have told you about things here on earth, and you do not believe me. So you will not believe me if I tell you about things of heaven. The only one who has ever gone up to heaven is the One who came down from heaven—the Son of Man.

"Just as Moses lifted up the snake in the desert, the Son of Man must also be lifted up. So that everyone who believes can have eternal life in him.

"God loved the world so much that he gave his one and only Son so that whoever believes in him may not be lost, but have eternal life. God did not send his Son into the world to judge the world guilty, but to save the world through him. People who believe in God's Son are not judged guilty. Those who do not believe have already been judged guilty, because they have not believed in God's one and only Son. They are judged by this fact: The Light has come into the world, but they did not want light. They wanted darkness, because they were doing evil things. All who do evil hate the light and will not come to the light, because it will show all the evil things they do. But those who follow the true way come to the light, and it shows that the things they do were done through God."

—JOHN 3:1–21

What Only God Can Do

I t's a fact of the farm. The most fertile ground remains barren if no
seed is sown.

Apparently Nicodemus didn't know that. He thought the soil could
bear fruit with no seeds. He was big on the farmer's part but forgetful
of the seed's part. He was a legalist. And that is how a legalist thinks. A
legalist prepares the soil but forgets the seed.

Nicodemus came about his legalism honestly. He was a Pharisee.

Pharisees taught that faith was an outside job. What you wore, how
you acted, the title you carried, the sound of your prayers, the amount
of your gifts—all these were the Pharisees' measure of spirituality.

Had they been farmers, they would have had the most attractive
acreage in the region—painted silos and sparkling equipment. The
fences would have been whitewashed and clean. The soil overturned
and watered.

Had they been farmers, they would have spent hours in the coffee
shop discussing the theory of farming. Is it best to fertilize before or
after a rain? Do you fallow a field every other year or every third year?
Should a farmer wear overalls or jeans? Cowboy hats or baseball caps?

The Pharisees had only one problem. For all their discussion
about the right techniques, they harvested little fruit. In fact, one
untrained Galilean had borne more fruit in a few short months than
all the Pharisees had in a generation. This made them jealous. Angry.
Condescending. And they dealt with him by ignoring his results and
insulting his methods.

That is, all the Pharisees except Nicodemus. He was curious. No,
more than curious, he was stirred; stirred by the way people listened to
Jesus. They listened as if he were the only one with truth. As if he were
a prophet.

Nicodemus was stirred by what he saw Jesus do. Like the time Jesus stormed into the temple and overturned the tables of the money changers. Nicodemus once knew such passion. But that was a long time ago—before the titles, before the robes, before the rules.

Nicodemus is drawn to the carpenter, but he can't be seen with him. Nicodemus is on the high court. He can't approach Jesus in the day. So Nicodemus goes to meet him at night. He goes in the darkness.

Appropriate. For legalism offers no light.

Nicodemus begins with courtesies. "Teacher, we know you are a teacher sent from God, because no one can do the miracles you do unless God is with him" (John 3:2).

Jesus disregards the compliment. "I tell you the truth, unless you are born again, you cannot be in God's kingdom" (v. 3).

No chitchat here. No idle talk. Straight to the point. Straight to the heart. Straight to the problem. Jesus knows the heart of the legalist is hard. You can't crack it with feathery accolades. You need a chisel. So Jesus hammers away:

> You can't help the blind by turning up the light, Nicodemus.
> You can't help the deaf by turning up the music, Nicodemus.
> You can't change the inside by decorating the outside, Nicodemus.
> You can't grow fruit without seed, Nicodemus.
> You must be born again.
> Whack! Whack! Whack!

The meeting between Jesus and Nicodemus was more than an encounter between two religious figures. It was a collision between two philosophies. Two opposing views on salvation.

Nicodemus thought the person did the work; Jesus says God does the work. Nicodemus thought it was a trade-off. Jesus says it is a gift. Nicodemus thought man's job was to earn it. Jesus says man's job is to accept it.

These two views encompass all views. All the world religions can be placed in one of two camps: legalism or grace. Humankind does it or

God does it. Salvation as a wage based on deeds done—or salvation as a gift based on Christ's death.

A legalist believes the supreme force behind salvation is you. If you look right, speak right, and belong to the right segment of the right group, you will be saved. The brunt of responsibility doesn't lie within God; it lies within you.

The result? The outside sparkles. The talk is good and the step is true. But look closely. Listen carefully. Something is missing. What is it? Joy. What's there? Fear. (That you won't do enough.) Arrogance. (That you have done enough.) Failure. (That you have made a mistake.)

Legalism is a dark world.

If you have never known the crush of legalism, be grateful. You have been spared.

Others of you haven't. You know that legalism is slow torture, suffocation of the spirit, amputation of one's dreams. Legalism is just enough religion to keep you but not enough to nourish you.

So you starve. Your teachers don't know where to go for food, so you starve together. Your diet is rules and standards. No vitamins. No taste. No zest. Just bland, predictable religion.

Reminds me of a group I was in as a youngster. When I was eight years old I was part of a boys' choir. We met two evenings a week for two hours. We wore blazers and sang at banquets. We even went on the road.

Curiously, our instructor was an ex–drill sergeant. Before he ran a boys' choir, he ran a boot camp. And some of the previous spilled over into the latter. Every evening during rehearsals, we took a marching break. We'd go outside and march in formation. He gave the commands, and we did the turns.

"Hut, two, three, four. Hut, two, three, four."

At first, I didn't question the practice. I didn't have the courage. I was intimidated by the man. Finally, I summoned enough guts to ask the kid beside me to explain the marching.

"Why are we doing this?"

"I don't know."

"Where are we going?"

"I don't know."

No one did. For two years we marched two nights every week. But no one knew where we were going and no one knew why. We just knew that if we wanted to sing we'd better stay in step.

That's legalism.

It's rigid. It's uniform. It's mechanical—and it's not from God.

Can I give you the down and dirty about legalism?

Legalism doesn't need God. Legalism is the search for innocence—not forgiveness. It's a systematic process of defending self, explaining self, exalting self, and justifying self. Legalists are obsessed with self—not God.

Legalism:

> Turns my opinion into your burden. There is only room for one opinion in this boat. And guess who is wrong!
>
> Turns my opinion into your boundary. Your opposing opinion makes me question not only your right to have fellowship with me but also your salvation.
>
> Turns my opinion into your obligation. Christians must toe the company line. Your job isn't to think; it's to march.

If you want to be in the group, stay in step and don't ask questions.

Nicodemus knew how to march, but he longed to sing. He knew there was something more, but he didn't know where to find it. So he went to Jesus.

He went at night because he feared the displeasure of his peers. Legalism puts the fear of man in you. It makes you approval-hungry. You become keenly aware of what others will say and think, and you do what it takes to please them. Conformity is not fun, but it's safe. The uniform doesn't fit, but it's approved, so you wear it. You don't know why you are marching or where you are going—but who are you to ask questions? So you stay in step and plod down the path of least resistance.

And if you dare explore another trail, you must do so at night, like

Nicodemus did. He snuck through the shadows and crept through the ebony streets until he stood in the presence of Christ. In the conversation, Nicodemus, the renowned teacher of the law, speaks only three times: once to compliment and twice to question. After a lifetime of weighing the tittles of Scripture in the scale of logic, the scholar becomes suddenly silent as Jesus opens the gate and the light of grace floods the catacomb.

Jesus begins by revealing the source of spirituality: "Human life comes from human parents, but spiritual life comes from the Spirit" (v. 6).

Spiritual life is not a human endeavor. It is rooted in and orchestrated by the Holy Spirit. Every spiritual achievement is created and energized by God.

Spirituality, Jesus says, comes not from church attendance or good deeds or correct doctrine, but from heaven itself. Such words must have set Nicodemus back on his heels. But Jesus was just getting started.

"The wind blows where it wants to and you hear the sound of it, but you don't know where the wind comes from or where it is going. It is the same with every person who is born from the Spirit" (v. 8).

Ever had a gust of wind come to you for help? Ever seen a windstorm on the side of the road catching its breath? No, you haven't. The wind doesn't seek our aid. Wind doesn't even reveal its destiny. It's silent and invisible, and so is the Spirit.

By now Nicodemus was growing edgy. Such light is too bright for his eyes. We religious teachers like to control and manage. We like to define and outline. Structure and clarity are the friend of the preacher. But they aren't always the protocol of God.

Salvation is God's business. Grace is his idea, his work, and his expense. He offers it to whom he desires, when he desires. Our job in the process is to inform the people, not to screen the people.

The question must have been written all over Nicodemus's face. Why would God do this? What would motivate him to offer such a gift? What Jesus told Nicodemus, Nicodemus never could have imagined. The motive behind the gift of new birth? Love. "God loved the world so much that he gave his one and only Son so that whoever believes in him may not be lost, but have eternal life" (v. 16).

Nicodemus has never heard such words. Never. He has had many discussions of salvation. But this is the first in which no rules were given. No system was offered. No code or ritual. "Everyone who believes can have eternal life in him," Jesus told him. Could God be so generous? Even in the darkness of night, the amazement is seen on Nicodemus's face. *Everyone who believes can have eternal life.* Not "everyone who achieves." Not "everyone who succeeds." Not "everyone who agrees." But "everyone who believes."

Note how God liberates the legalist. Observe the tender firmness of his touch. Like a master farmer, he shoveled away the crusty soil until a moist, fertile spot was found, and there he planted a seed, a seed of grace.

Did it bear fruit? Read the following and see for yourself.

Nicodemus, who earlier had come to Jesus at night, went with Joseph. He brought about seventy-five pounds of myrrh and aloes. These two men took Jesus' body and wrapped it with the spices in pieces of linen cloth, which is how [Jewish people] bury the dead. In the place where Jesus was crucified, there was a garden. In the garden was a new tomb that had never been used before. The men laid Jesus in that tomb. (John 19:39–42)

Strange how a man can go full circle in the kingdom. The one who'd come at night now appears in the day. The one who crept through the shadows to meet Jesus now comes to the cross to serve Jesus. And the one who'd received the seed of grace now plants the greatest seed of all—the seed of eternal life.

QUESTIONS FOR REFLECTION AND DISCUSSION

1. Read John 3:2. Why do you think Jesus ignored Nicodemus's comment and instead responded, "I tell you the truth, unless you are born again, you cannot be in God's kingdom"?

2. Comment on the following statement: "Legalism is slow torture, suffocation of the spirit, amputation of one's dreams." If you have ever felt legalism's grip, explain your experience.

3. Read Colossians 2:20–23. Why do you think we are so easily drawn back into legalism? What is the only way to stay free of it?

4. Read Galatians 5:1–6. How does this passage teach that salvation cannot be achieved through a mixture of faith and deeds?

5. How does John 19:39–42 prove that Nicodemus finally escaped the trap of legalism? How did he escape this grip?

Chapter 12

ANANIAS AND SAUL

Brother Saul, the Lord Jesus, who appeared to you on the road as you came, has sent me that you may receive your sight and be filled with the Holy Spirit.

—ACTS 9:17 NKJV

DON'T WRITE OFF ANYONE

Ananias hurries through the narrow Damascus streets.[1] His dense and bristling beard does not hide his serious face. Friends call as he passes, but he doesn't pause. He murmurs as he goes, "Saul? *Saul?* No way. Can't be true."

He wonders if he misheard the instructions. Wonders if he should turn around and inform his wife. Wonders if he should stop and tell someone where he is headed in case he never returns. But he doesn't. Friends would call him a fool. His wife would tell him not to go.

But he has to. He scampers through the courtyard of chickens, towering camels, and little donkeys. He steps past the shop of the tailor and doesn't respond to the greeting of the tanner. He keeps moving until he reaches the street called Straight. The inn has low arches and large rooms with mattresses. Nice by Damascus standards, the place of choice for any person of significance or power, and Saul is certainly both.

Ananias and the other Christians have been preparing for him. Some of the disciples have left the city. Others have gone into hiding. Saul's reputation as a Christian-killer preceded him. But the idea of Saul the Christ follower?

That was the message of the vision. Ananias replays it one more time.

"Arise and go to the street called Straight, and inquire at the house of Judas for one called Saul of Tarsus, for behold, he is praying. And in a vision he has seen a man named Ananias coming in and putting his hand on him, so that he might receive his sight" (Acts 9:11–12 NKJV).

Ananias nearly choked on his matzo. *This isn't possible!* He reminded God of Saul's hard heart. "I have heard from many about this man, how much harm he has done to Your saints in Jerusalem" (v. 13 NKJV). Saul a *Christian*? Sure, as soon as a turtle learns to two-step.

But God wasn't teasing. "Go, for he is a chosen vessel of Mine to bear My name before Gentiles, kings, and the children of Israel" (v. 15 NKJV).

Ananias rehashes the words as he walks. The name Saul doesn't couple well with *chosen vessel*. Saul the thickhead—yes. Saul the critic— okay. But Saul the chosen vessel? Ananias shakes his head at the thought. By now he is halfway down Straight Street and seriously considering turning around and going home. He would have, except the two guards spot him.

"What brings you here?" they shout from the second story. They stand at attention. Their faces are wintry with unrest.

Ananias knows who they are—soldiers from the temple. Traveling companions of Saul.

"I've been sent to help the rabbi."

They lower their spears. "We hope you can. Something has happened to him. He doesn't eat or drink. Scarcely speaks."

Ananias can't turn back now. He ascends the stone stairs. The guards step aside, and Ananias steps into the doorway. He gasps at what he sees. A gaunt man sitting cross-legged on the floor, half shadowed by a shaft of sunlight. Hollow-cheeked and dry-lipped, he rocks back and forth, groaning a prayer.

"How long has he been like this?"

"Three days."

Saul's head sits large on his shoulders. He has a beaked nose and a bushy ridge for eyebrows. The food on the plate and the water in the cup sit untouched on the floor. His eyes stare out of their sockets in the direction of an open window. A crusty film covers them. Saul doesn't even wave the flies away from his face. Ananias hesitates. If this is a setup, he is history. If not, the moment is.

This encounter deserves something special: a drumroll, a stained-glass reenactment in a church window, some pages in a book called *You, on a Pew?* Before we read about Augustine and the child's voice or C. S. Lewis and the Inklings, we need to read about Saul, stubborn Saul, and the disciple who took a chance on him.

No one could fault Ananias's reluctance. Saul saw Christians as couriers of a plague. He stood near the high priest at Stephen's trial. He watched over the coats of stone-throwers at the execution. He nodded in approval at Stephen's final breath. And when the Sanhedrin needed a hit man to terrorize the church, Saul stepped forward. He became the Angel of Death. He descended on the Christians in a fury "uttering threats with every breath" (Acts 9:1 NLT). He "persecuted the church of God beyond measure and tried to destroy it" (Gal. 1:13 NKJV).

Ananias knew what Saul had done to the church in Jerusalem. What he was about to learn, however, is what Jesus had done to Saul on the road to Damascus.

The trip was Saul's idea. The city had seen large numbers of conversions. When word of the revival reached Saul, he made his request: "Send me." So the fiery young Hebrew left Jerusalem on his first missionary journey, hell-bent on stopping the church. The journey to Damascus was a long one, one hundred and fifty miles. Saul likely rode horseback, careful to bypass the Gentile villages. This was a holy journey.

It was also a hot journey. The lowland between Mount Hermon and Damascus could melt silver. The sun struck like spears; the heat made waves out of the horizon. Somewhere on this thirsty trail, Jesus knocked Saul to the ground and asked him, "Saul, Saul, why are you persecuting Me?" (Acts 9:4 NKJV).

Saul jammed his fists into his eye sockets as if they were filled with sand. He rolled onto his knees and lowered his head down to the earth. "'Who are You, Lord?' Then the Lord said, 'I am Jesus, whom you are persecuting'" (v. 5 NKJV). When Saul lifted his head to look, the living centers of his eyes had vanished. He was blind. He had the vacant stare of a Roman statue.

His guards rushed to help. They led him to the Damascus inn and walked with him up the stairwell.

By the time Ananias arrives, blind Saul has begun to see Jesus in a different light.

Ananias enters and sits on the stone floor. He takes the hand of the had-been terrorist and feels it tremble. He observes Saul's quivering lips. Taking note of the sword and spear resting in the corner, Ananias realizes Christ has already done the work. All that remains is for Ananias to show Saul the next step. "Brother Saul . . ." (How sweet those words must have sounded. Saul surely wept upon hearing them.)

> Brother Saul, the Lord Jesus, who appeared to you on the road as you came, has sent me that you may receive your sight and be filled with the Holy Spirit. (v. 17 NKJV)

Tears rush like a tide against the crusts on Saul's eyes. The scaly covering loosens and falls away. He blinks and sees the face of his new friend.

Within the hour he's stepping out of the waters of baptism. Within a few days he's preaching in a synagogue. The first of a thousand sermons. Saul soon becomes Paul, and Paul preaches from the hills of Athens, pens letters from the bowels of prisons, and ultimately sires a genealogy of theologians, including Aquinas, Luther, and Calvin.

God used Paul to touch the world. But he first used Ananias to touch Paul. Has God given you a similar assignment? Has God given you a Saul?

A mother recently talked to me about her son. He's serving time in a maximum-security unit for robbery. Everyone else, even his father, has given up on the young man. But his mom has a different outlook. She really thinks her son's best years are ahead of him. "He's a good boy," she said firmly. "When he gets out of there, he's going to make something out of his life."

Another Saul, another Ananias.

I ran into a friend in a bookstore. He recently celebrated his fiftieth wedding anniversary. He teared up as he described the saint he married and the jerk his wife married. "I didn't believe in God. I didn't treat people with respect. Six weeks into the marriage, I came home one day to find her crying in the bathtub about the mistake she had made. But she never gave up on me."

Another Saul, another Ananias.

And you? Everyone else has written off your Saul. "He's too far gone." "She's too hard . . . too addicted . . . too old . . . too cold." No one gives your Saul a prayer. But you are beginning to realize that maybe God is at work behind the scenes. Maybe it's too soon to throw in the towel . . . You begin to believe.

Don't resist these thoughts.

Joseph didn't. His brothers sold him into Egyptian slavery. Yet he welcomed them into his palace.

David didn't. King Saul had a vendetta against David, but David had a soft spot for Saul. He called him "the LORD's anointed" (1 Sam. 24:10 NKJV).

Hosea didn't. His wife, Gomer, was queen of the red-light district, but Hosea kept his front door open. And she came home.

Of course, no one believed in people more than Jesus did. He saw something in Peter worth developing, in the adulterous woman worth forgiving, and in John worth harnessing. He saw something in the thief on the cross, and what he saw was worth saving. And in the life of a wild-eyed, bloodthirsty extremist, he saw an apostle of grace. He believed in Saul. And he believed in Saul through Ananias.

"Brother Saul, the Lord Jesus, who appeared to you on the road as you came, has sent me that you may receive your sight and be filled with the Holy Spirit" (Acts 9:17 NKJV).

Don't give up on your Saul. When others write him off, give him another chance. Stay strong. Call him *brother*. Call her *sister*. Tell your Saul about Jesus, and pray. And remember this: God never sends you where he hasn't already been. By the time you reach your Saul, who knows what you'll find.

My favorite Ananias-type story involves a couple of college roommates. The Ananias of the pair was a tolerant soul. He tolerated his friend's late-night drunkenness, midnight throw-ups, and all-day sleep-ins. He didn't complain when his friend disappeared for the weekend or smoked cigarettes in the car. He could have requested a roommate who went to church more or cursed less or cared about something other than impressing girls.

But he hung with his personal Saul, seeming to think that something good could happen if the guy could pull his life together. So he kept cleaning up the mess, inviting his roommate to church, and covering his back.

I don't remember a bright light or a loud voice. I've never traveled a desert road to Damascus. But I distinctly remember Jesus knocking me off my perch and flipping on the light. It took four semesters, but Steve's example and Jesus' message finally got through.

So if this book lifts your spirit, you might thank God for my Ananias, Steve Green. Even more, you might listen to that voice in your heart and look on your map for a street called Straight.

QUESTIONS FOR REFLECTION AND DISCUSSION

1. Name a very public or famous person whom nobody would expect to convert to Christianity. Why does it seem so unlikely that the person would become a Christian?

2. Share a story either about yourself or someone whom you know personally who made an unexpected radical conversion to God.

3. "Has God given you a Saul?" Is there someone in your life whom most people have given up on and dismissed? How could you be an Ananias for that person?

4. What does Scripture say about reaching out to those in need? How can you be more sensitive to the Father's promptings in this area?

5. How would you describe your conversion? Was it sudden or gradual? What are you doing to help others experience conversion?

Chapter 13

⚜

DAVID

Then David said to Nathan, "I have sinned against the LORD."
Nathan replied, "The LORD has taken away your sin. You are not going to die."

—2 SAMUEL 12:13 NIV

COLOSSAL COLLAPSES

What will the Vatican give for the pope's name? Rogers Cadenhead sought an answer. Upon the death of Pope John Paul, this self-described "domain hoarder" registered www.BenedictXVI.com before the new pope's name was announced. Cadenhead secured it before Rome knew they needed it.

The right domain name can prove lucrative. Another name, www.PopeBenedictXVI.com, surpassed sixteen thousand dollars on eBay. Cadenhead, however, didn't want money. A Catholic himself, he's happy for the church to own the name. "I'm going to try and avoid angering 1.1 billion Catholics and my grandmother," he quipped.

He would like something in return, though. In exchange, Cadenhead sought

1. "one of those hats";
2. "a free stay at the Vatican hotel";
3. "complete absolution, no questions asked, for the third week of March 1987."[1]

Makes you wonder what happened that week, doesn't it? It may remind you of a week of your own. Most of us have one, or more.

A folly-filled summer, a month off track, days gone wild. If a box of tapes existed documenting every second of your life, which tapes would you burn? Do you have a season in which you indulged, imbibed, or inhaled?

King David did. Could a collapse be more colossal than his? He seduces and impregnates Bathsheba, murders her husband, and deceives his general and soldiers. Then he marries her. She bears the child.

The cover-up appears complete. The casual observer detects no cause for concern. David has a new wife and a happy life. All seems well on the throne. But all is not well in David's heart. Guilt simmers. He will later describe this season of secret sin in graphic terms:

When I kept it all inside,
 my bones turned to powder,
 my words became daylong groans.
The pressure never let up;
 all the juices of my life dried up. (Ps. 32:3–4 MSG)

David's soul resembles a Canadian elm in winter. Barren. Fruitless. Gray-shrouded. His harp hangs unstrung. His hope hibernates. The guy is a walking wreck. His "third week of March" stalks him like a pack of wolves. He can't escape it. Why? Because God keeps bringing it up.

Underline the last verse of 2 Samuel chapter 11: "The thing that David had done displeased the LORD" (v. 27 NKJV). With these words the narrator introduces a new character into the David and Bathsheba drama: God. Thus far, he's been absent from the text, unmentioned in the story.

David seduces—no mention of God. David plots—no mention of God. Uriah buried, Bathsheba married—no mention of God. God is not spoken to and does not speak. The first half of verse 27 lures the reader into a faux happy ending: Bathsheba "became David's wife and gave birth to his son." They decorate the nursery and pick names out of a magazine. Nine months pass. A son is born. And we conclude: David dodged a bullet. Angels dropped this story into the file marked "Boys will be boys." God turned a blind eye. Yet, just when we think so and David hopes so . . . Someone steps from behind the curtain and takes center stage. "The thing that David had done displeased the LORD."

God will be silent no more. The name not mentioned until the final verse of chapter 11 dominates chapter 12. David, the "sender," sits while God takes control.

God sends Nathan to David. Nathan is a prophet, a preacher, a

White House chaplain of sorts. The man deserves a medal for going to the king. He knows what happened to Uriah. David had killed an innocent soldier . . . What will he do with a confronting preacher?

Still, Nathan goes. Rather than declare the deed, he relates a story about a poor man with one sheep. David instantly connects. He shepherded flocks before he led people. He knows poverty. He's the youngest son of a family too poor to hire a shepherd. Nathan tells David how the poor shepherd loved this sheep—holding her in his own lap, feeding her from his own plate. She was all he had.

Enter, as the story goes, the rich jerk. A traveler stops by his mansion, so a feast is in order. Rather than slaughter a sheep from his own flock, the rich man sends his bodyguards to steal the poor man's animal. They Hummer onto his property, snatch the lamb, and fire up the barbecue.

As David listens, hair rises on his neck. He grips the arms of the throne. He renders a verdict without a trial: fish bait by nightfall. "The man who has done this shall surely die! And he shall restore fourfold for the lamb, because he did this thing and because he had no pity" (2 Sam. 12:5–6 NKJV).

Oh, David. You never saw it coming, did you? You never saw Nathan erecting the gallows or throwing the rope over the beam. You never felt him tie your hands behind your back, lead you up the steps, and stand you squarely over the trap door. Only when he squeezed the noose around your neck did you gulp. Only when Nathan tightened the rope with four three-letter words:

"You are the man!" (v. 7 NKJV).

David's face pales; his Adam's apple bounces. A bead of sweat forms on his forehead. He slinks back in his chair. He makes no defense. He utters no response. He has nothing to say. God, however, is just clearing his throat. Through Nathan he proclaims:

I made you king over Israel. I freed you from the fist of Saul. I gave you your master's daughter and other wives to have and to hold. I gave you both Israel and Judah. And if that hadn't been enough, I'd have gladly thrown in much more. So why have you treated the word of God with brazen contempt, doing this great evil? You murdered Uriah the Hittite, then took his wife as your wife. Worse, you killed him with an Ammonite sword! (vv. 7–9 MSG)

God's words reflect hurt, not hate; bewilderment, not belittlement. Your flock fills the hills. Why rob? Beauty populates your palace. Why take from someone else? Why would the wealthy steal? David has no excuse.

So God levies a sentence.

Now, therefore, the sword will never depart from your house, because you despised me and took the wife of Uriah the Hittite to be your own.

This is what the LORD says: "Out of your own household I am going to bring calamity upon you. Before your very eyes I will take your wives and give them to one who is close to you, and he will lie with your wives in broad daylight. You did it in secret, but I will do this thing in broad daylight before all Israel." (vv. 10–12 NIV)

From this day forward, turmoil and tragedy mark David's family. Even the child of this adultery will die (v. 18). He must. Surrounding nations now question the holiness of David's God. David had soiled God's reputation, blemished God's honor. And God, who jealously guards his glory, punishes David's public sin in a public fashion. The infant perishes. The king of Israel discovers the harsh truth of Numbers 32:23: ". . . you can be sure that your sin will track you down" (MSG).

Have you found this to be true? Does your stubborn week of March 1987 hound you? Infect you? Colossal collapses won't leave us alone. They surface like a boil on the skin.

My brother had one once. In his middle school years he contracted a case of the boils. Poisonous pus rose on the back of his neck like a tiny Mount St. Helens. My mom, a nurse, knew what the boil needed—a good squeezing. Two thumbs every morning. The more she pressed, the more he screamed. But she wouldn't stop until the seed of the boil popped out.

Gee, Max, thanks for the beautiful image.

I'm sorry to be so graphic, but I need to press this point. You think my mom was tough . . . Try the hands of God. Unconfessed sins sit on our hearts like festering boils, poisoning, expanding. And God, with gracious thumbs, applies the pressure:

"The way of the transgressor is hard" (Prov. 13:15 ASV).

"Those who plow evil and sow trouble reap evil and trouble" (Job 4:8 MSG).

God takes your sleep, your peace. He takes your rest. Want to know why? Because he wants to take away your sin. Can a mom do nothing as toxins invade her child? Can God sit idly as sin poisons his? He will not rest until we do what David did: confess our fault. "Then David said to Nathan, 'I have sinned against the LORD.' Nathan replied, 'The LORD has taken away your sin. You are not going to die' " (2 Sam. 12:13 NIV).

Interesting. David sentenced the imaginary sheep stealer to death. God is more merciful. He put away David's sin. Rather than cover it up, he lifted it up and put it away. "As far as the east is from the west, so far has he removed our transgressions from us. As a father has compassion on his children, so the LORD has compassion on those who fear him" (Ps. 103:12–13 NIV).

It took David a year. It took a surprise pregnancy, the death of a soldier, the persuasion of a preacher, and the probing and pressing of God, but David's hard heart finally softened, and he confessed: "I have sinned against the LORD" (2 Sam. 12:13 NIV).

And God did with the sin what he does with yours and mine—he put it away.

It's time for you to put your "third week of March 1987" to rest.

Assemble a meeting of three parties: you, God, and your memory. Place the mistake before the judgment seat of God. Let him condemn it, let him pardon it, and let him put it away.

He will. And you don't have to own the pope's name for him to do so.

QUESTIONS FOR REFLECTION AND DISCUSSION

1. Max writes, "David seduces—no mention of God. David plots—no mention of God. Uriah buried, Bathsheba married—no mention of God. God is not spoken to and does not speak." Why do you think God does not speak to David during all this evil activity? Why is he silent?

2. Read Psalm 32:3–5. How did David feel during the time he tried to cover up his sin? How did God respond when David finally confessed his sin?

3. When you think of hidden sins in your life, do you ever fear God will not forgive you or that you have sinned so badly you can never be used by God? Read 2 Samuel 11:27–12:25. What was the first thing David did right after many months of willful rebellion (12:13)? How did God respond to him?

4. Have you ever suffered a colossal collapse? If so, what steps did you take to recover from it?

5. Is there some sin in your recent past that you have yet to name, confess, and abandon? If so, as Max says, "Place the mistake before the judgment seat of God. Let him condemn it, let him pardon it, and let him put it away."

Chapter 14

JESUS'
BROTHERS

My true brother and sister and mother are those who do what God wants.

—MARK 3:35

FEUDIN' FAMILIES
FINDING PEACE

Give me a word picture to describe a relative in your life who really bugs you."

I was asking the question of a half-dozen friends sitting around a lunch table. They all gave me one of those what-in-the-world? expressions. So I explained.

"I keep meeting people who can't deal with somebody in their family. Either their mother-in-law is a witch or their uncle is a bum or they have a father who treats them like they were never born."

Now their heads nodded. We were connecting. And the word pictures started coming.

"I've got a description," one volunteered. "A parasite on my neck. My wife has this brother who never works and always expects us to provide."

"A cactus wearing a silk shirt," said another. "It's my mother. She looks nice. Everyone thinks she's the greatest, but get close to her and she is prickly, dry, and . . . thirsty for life."

"A marble column," was the way another described an aunt. Dignified, noble, but high and hard.

"Tar baby in Br'er Rabbit," someone responded. Everyone understood the reference except me. I didn't remember the story of Br'er Rabbit. I asked for the short version. Wily Fox played a trick on Br'er Rabbit. The fox made a doll out of tar and stuck it on the side of the road. When Rabbit saw the tar baby, he thought it was a person and stopped to visit.

It was a one-sided conversation. The tar baby's silence bothered the rabbit. He couldn't stand to be next to someone and not communicate with him. So in his frustration he hit the tar baby and stuck to it. He hit the tar baby again with the other hand and, you guessed it, the other hand got stuck.

"That's how we are with difficult relatives," my fable-using friend explained. "We're stuck to someone we can't communicate with."

Stuck is right. It's not as if they are neighbors you can move away from or employees you can fire. They are family. And you can choose your friends, but you can't . . . well, you know.

Odds are, you probably know very well.

You've probably got a tar baby in your life, someone you can't talk to and can't walk away from. A mother who whines, an uncle who slurps his soup, or a sister who flaunts her figure. A dad who is still waiting for you to get a real job or a mother-in-law who wonders why her daughter married you.

Tar-baby relationships—stuck together but falling apart.

It's like a crammed and jammed elevator. People thrust together by chance on a short journey, saying as little as possible. The only difference is you'll eventually get off the elevator and never see these folks again—not so with difficult relatives. Family reunions, Christmas, Thanksgiving, weddings, funerals—they'll be there.

And you'll be there sorting through the tough questions. Why does life get so *relatively* difficult? If we expect anyone to be sensitive to our needs, it is our family members. When we hurt physically, we want our family to respond. When we struggle emotionally, we want our family to know.

But sometimes they act like they don't know. Sometimes they act like they don't care.

In her book *Irregular People*, Joyce Landorf tells of a woman in her thirties who learned that she needed a mastectomy. She and her mother seldom communicated, so the daughter was apprehensive about telling her. One day over lunch, she decided to reveal the news. "Mother, I just learned that I am going to have a mastectomy."

The mother was silent. The daughter asked her if she had heard. The mother nodded her head. Then she calmly dismissed the subject by say-ing, "You know your sister has the best recipe for chicken enchiladas."

What can you do when those closest to you keep their distance? When you can get along with others, but you and your kin can't?

Does Jesus have anything to say about dealing with difficult rela-tives? Is there an example of Jesus bringing peace to a painful family? Yes, there is.

His own.

It may surprise you to know that Jesus had a difficult family. It may surprise you to know that Jesus had a family at all! You may not be aware that Jesus had brothers and sisters. He did. Quoting Jesus' home-town critics, Mark wrote, "[Jesus] is just the carpenter, the son of Mary and the brother of James, Joseph, Judas, and Simon. And his sisters are here with us" (v. 3).

And it may surprise you to know that his family was less than perfect. They were. If your family doesn't appreciate you, take heart, neither did Jesus'. "A prophet is honored everywhere except in his home-town and with his own people and in his own home" (v. 4).

I wonder what he meant when he said those last five words. He went to the synagogue where he was asked to speak. The people were proud that this hometown boy had done well—until they heard what he said. He referred to himself as the Messiah, the one to fulfill prophecy.

Their response? "Isn't this Joseph's son?" Translation? This is no Messiah! He's just like us! He's the plumber's kid from down the street. He's the accountant on the third floor. He's the construction worker who used to date my sister. God doesn't speak through familiar people.

One minute he was a hero, the next a heretic. Look what happens next. "They got up, forced Jesus out of town, and took him to the edge of the cliff on which the town was built. They planned to throw him off the edge, but Jesus walked through the crowd and went on his way" (Luke 4:29–30).

What an ugly moment! Jesus' neighborhood friends tried to kill him. But even uglier than what we see is what we don't see. Notice what is missing from this verse. Note what words should be there, but aren't. "They planned to throw him over the cliff, but Jesus' brothers came and stood up for him."

We'd like to read that, but we can't because it doesn't say that. That's not what happened. When Jesus was in trouble, his brothers were invisible.

They weren't always invisible, however. There was a time when they spoke. There was a time when they were seen with him in public. Not because they were proud of him but because they were ashamed of him. "His family . . . went to get him because they thought he was out of his mind" (Mark 3:21).

Jesus' siblings thought their brother was a lunatic. They weren't proud—they were embarrassed!

"He's off the deep end, Mom. You should hear what people are saying about him."

"People say he's loony."

"Yeah, somebody asked me why we don't do something about him."

"It's a good thing Dad isn't around to see what Jesus is doing."

Hurtful words spoken by those closest to Jesus.

Here are some more:

So Jesus' brothers said to him, "You should leave here and go to Judea so your followers there can see the miracles you do. Anyone who wants to be well known does not hide what he does. If you are doing these things, show yourself to the world." (Even Jesus' brothers did not believe in him.) (John 7:3–5)

Listen to the sarcasm in those words! They drip with ridicule. How does Jesus put up with these guys? How can you believe in yourself when those who know you best don't? How can you move forward when your family wants to pull you back? When you and your family have two different agendas, what do you do?

Jesus gives us some answers.

It's worth noting that he didn't try to control his family's behavior, nor did he let their behavior control his. He didn't demand that they agree with him. He didn't sulk when they insulted him. He didn't make it his mission to try to please them.

Each of us has a fantasy that our family will be like the Waltons, an expectation that our dearest friends will be our next of kin. Jesus didn't have that expectation. Look how he defined his family: "My true brother and sister and mother are those who do what God wants" (Mark 3:35).

When Jesus' brothers didn't share his convictions, he didn't try to force them. He recognized that his spiritual family could provide what his physical family didn't. If Jesus himself couldn't force his family to share his convictions, what makes you think you can force yours?

We can't control the way our family responds to us. When it comes to the behavior of others toward us, our hands are tied. We have to move beyond the naive expectation that if we do good, people will treat us right. The fact is they may and they may not—we cannot control how people respond to us.

If your father is a jerk, you could be the world's best daughter and he still won't tell you so.

If your aunt doesn't like your career, you could change jobs a dozen times and still never satisfy her.

If your sister is always complaining about what you got and she didn't, you could give her everything and she still may not change.

As long as you think you can control people's behavior toward you, you are held in bondage by their opinions. If you think you can control their opinion and their opinion isn't positive, then guess who you have to blame? Yourself.

It's a game with unfair rules and fatal finishes. Jesus didn't play it, nor should you.

We don't know if Joseph affirmed his son Jesus in his ministry—but we know God did: "This is my Son, whom I love, and I am very pleased with him" (Matt. 3:17).

I can't assure you that your family will ever give you the blessing you seek, but I know God will. Let God give you what your family doesn't. If your earthly father doesn't affirm you, then let your heavenly Father take his place.

How do you do that? By emotionally accepting God as your Father. You see, it's one thing to accept him as Lord, another to recognize him as Savior—but it's another matter entirely to accept him as Father.

To recognize God as Lord is to acknowledge that he is sovereign and supreme in the universe. To accept him as Savior is to accept his gift of salvation offered on the cross. To regard him as Father is to go a step further. Ideally, a father is the one in your life who provides and protects. That is exactly what God has done.

He has provided for your needs (Matt. 6:25–34). He has protected you from harm (Ps. 139:5). He has adopted you (Eph. 1:5). And he has given you his name (1 John 3:1).

God has proven himself as a faithful father. Now it falls to us to be trusting children. Let God give you what your family doesn't. Let him fill the void others have left. Rely upon him for your affirmation and encouragement. Look at Paul's words: "You are God's child, and *God will give you the blessing he promised*, because you are his child" (Gal. 4:7; emphasis added).

Having your family's approval is desirable but not necessary for happiness and not always possible. Jesus did not let the difficult dynamic of his family overshadow his call from God. And because he didn't, this chapter has a happy ending.

What happened to Jesus' family?

Mine with me a golden nugget hidden in a vein of the book of Acts. "Then [the disciples] went back to Jerusalem from the Mount of Olives. . . . They all continued praying together with some women, *including Mary the mother of Jesus, and Jesus' brothers*" (Acts 1:12, 14; emphasis added).

What a change! The ones who mocked him now worship him. The ones who pitied him now pray for him. What if Jesus had disowned them? Or worse still, what if he'd suffocated his family with his demand for change?

He didn't. He instead gave them space, time, and grace. And because he did, they changed. How much did they change? One brother became an apostle (Gal. 1:19) and others became missionaries (1 Cor. 9:5).

So don't lose heart. God still changes families. A tar baby today might be your dearest friend tomorrow.

Questions for Reflection and Discussion

1. Do you have any "tar-baby relatives"? If so, what makes it hard to communicate with them?

2. How does it make you feel that Jesus himself had a difficult family? What was your reaction when you first read this statement?

3. Go back through the chapter and list the many ways Jesus' family dishonored him. How did Jesus respond to these insults? What can we learn from these incidents?

4. Max writes, "It's worth noting that [Jesus] didn't try to control his family's behavior, nor did he let their behavior control his." In what ways is this an excellent principle for us?

5. How did the members of Jesus' family finally change in their appraisal of him? How can this give us hope?

Chapter 15

THE CRIPPLED MAN AT THE BEAUTIFUL GATE

Peter, with John at his side, looked him straight in the eye. . . .
He grabbed him by the right hand and pulled him up.

—ACTS 3:4, 7 MSG

SEE THE NEED;
TOUCH THE HURT

A gate called Beautiful. The man was anything but.

He couldn't walk but had to drag himself about on his knees. He passed his days among the contingent of real and pretend beggars who coveted the coins of the worshippers entering Solomon's court.

Peter and John were among them.

The needy man saw the apostles, lifted his voice, and begged for money. They had none to give, yet still they stopped. "Peter and John looked straight at him and said, 'Look at us!'" (Acts 3:4). They locked their eyes on his with such compassion that "he gave them his attention, expecting to receive something from them" (v. 5 NKJV). Peter and John issued no embarrassed glance, irritated shrug, or cynical dismissal but an honest look.

It is hard to look suffering in the face. Wouldn't we rather turn away? Stare in a different direction? Fix our gaze on fairer objects? Human hurt is not easy on the eyes. The dusty cheeks of the Pakistani refugee. The wide-eyed stare of the Peruvian orphan. Or the salt-and-pepper tangle of a beard worn by the drifter Stanley and I met in Pennsylvania.

Stanley Shipp served as a father to my young faith. He was thirty years my senior and blessed with a hawkish nose, thin lips, a rim of white hair, and a heart as big as the Midwest. His business cards, which he gave to those who requested and those who didn't, read simply, "Stanley Shipp—Your Servant."

I spent my first postcollege year under his tutelage. One of our trips took us to a small church in rural Pennsylvania for a conference. He and I happened to be the only two people at the building when a drifter, wearing alcohol like a cheap perfume, knocked on the door. He recited his victim spiel. Overqualified for work. Unqualified for pension. Lost bus ticket. Bad back. His kids in Kansas didn't care. If bad breaks were rock and roll, this guy was Elvis. I crossed my arms, smirked, and gave Stanley a get-a-load-of-this-guy glance.

Stanley didn't return it. He devoted every optic nerve to the drifter. Stanley saw no one else but him. *How long,* I remember wondering, *since anyone looked this fellow square in the face?*

The meandering saga finally stopped, and Stanley led the man into the church kitchen and prepared him a plate of food and a sack of groceries. As we watched him leave, Stanley blinked back a tear and responded to my unsaid thoughts. "Max, I know he's probably lying. But what if just one part of his story was true?"

We both saw the man. I saw right through him. Stanley saw deep into him. There is something fundamentally good about taking time to see a person.

Simon the Pharisee once disdained Jesus' kindness toward a woman of questionable character. So Jesus tested him: "Do you see this woman?" (Luke 7:44 NKJV).

Simon didn't. He saw a hussy, a streetwalker, a scamp. He didn't see the woman.

What do we see when we see . . .

- the figures beneath the overpass, encircling the fire in a fifty-five-gallon drum?
- the news clips of children in refugee camps?
- reports of 1.75 billion people who live on less than $1.25 a day?[1]

What do we see? "When He saw the multitudes, He was moved with compassion for them, because they were weary and scattered, like sheep having no shepherd" (Matt. 9:36 NKJV).

This word *compassion* is one of the oddest in Scripture. The New Testament Greek lexicon says this word means "to be moved as to one's bowels . . . (for the bowels were thought to be the seat of love and pity)."[2]

It shares a root system with *splanchnology*, the study of the visceral parts. Compassion, then, is a movement deep within—a kick in the gut.

Perhaps that is why we turn away. Who can bear such an emotion? Especially when we can do nothing about it. Why look suffering in the face if we can't make a difference?

Yet what if we could? What if our attention could reduce someone's pain? This is the promise of the encounter.

Then Peter said, "Silver and gold I do not have, but what I do have I give you: In the name of Jesus Christ of Nazareth, rise up and walk." And he took him by the right hand and lifted him up, and immediately his feet and ankle bones received strength. So he, leaping up, stood and walked and entered the temple with them—walking, leaping, and praising God. (Acts 3:6–8 NKJV)

What if Peter had said, "Since I don't have any silver or gold, I'll keep my mouth shut"? But he didn't. He placed his mustard-seed-sized deed (a look and a touch) in the soil of God's love. And look what happened.

The thick, meaty hand of the fisherman reached for the frail, thin one of the beggar. Think Sistine Chapel and the high hand of God. One from above, the other from below. A holy helping hand. Peter lifted the man toward himself. The cripple swayed like a newborn calf finding its balance. It appeared as if the man would fall, but he didn't. He stood. And as he stood, he began to shout, and passersby began to stop. They stopped and watched the cripple skip.

Don't you think he did? Not at first, mind you. But after a careful step, then another few, don't you think he skipped a jig? Parading and waving the mat on which he had lived?

The crowd thickened around the trio. The apostles laughed as the beggar danced. Other beggars pressed toward the scene in their ragged coverings and tattered robes and cried out for their portion of a miracle.

"I want my healing! Touch me! Touch me!"

So Peter complied. He escorted them to the clinic of the Great

Physician and invited them to take a seat. "His name, . . . faith in His name, has made this man strong. . . . Repent therefore and be converted, that your sins may be blotted out, so that times of refreshing may come from the presence of the Lord" (vv. 16, 19 NKJV).

Blotted out is a translation of a Greek term that means "to obliterate" or "erase completely." Faith in Christ, Peter explained, leads to a clean slate with God. What Jesus did for the legs of this cripple, he does for our souls. Brand-new!

An honest look led to a helping hand that led to a conversation about eternity. Works done in God's name long outlive our earthly lives.

Let's be the people who stop at the gate. Let's look at the hurting until we hurt with them. No hurrying past, turning away, or shifting of eyes. No pretending or glossing over. Let's look at the face until we see the person.

A couple in our congregation lives with the heartbreaking reality that their son is homeless. He ran away when he was seventeen, and with the exception of a few calls from prison and one visit, his parents have had no contact with him for twenty years. His mom allowed me to interview her at a leadership gathering. As we prepared for the discussion, I asked her why she was willing to disclose her story.

"I want to change the way people see the homeless. I want them to stop seeing problems and begin seeing mothers' sons."

In certain Zulu areas of South Africa, people greet each other with a phrase that means "I see you."[3] Change begins with a genuine look.

And continues with a helping hand. I'm writing this chapter by a dim light in an Ethiopian hotel only a few miles and hours removed from a modern-day version of this story.

Bzuneh Tulema lives in a two-room, dirt-floored, cinder-block house at the end of a dirt road in the dry hills of Adama. Maybe three hundred square feet. He's painted the walls a pastel blue and hung two pictures of Jesus, one of which bears the caption "Jesus the Goos [sic] Shepherd." During our visit the air is hot, the smell of cow manure is pungent, and I don't dare inhale too deeply for fear I'll swallow a fly.

Across from me, Bzuneh beams. He wears a Nike cap with a crooked bill, a red jacket (in spite of furnace-level heat), and a gap-toothed smile. No king was ever prouder of a castle than he is of his four walls. As the thirty-five-year-old relates his story, I understand.

Just two years ago he was the town drunk. He drank away his first marriage and came within a prayer of doing the same with the second. He and his wife were so consumed with alcohol that they farmed out their kids to neighbors and resigned themselves to a drunken demise.

But then someone saw them. Like Peter and John saw the beggar, members of an area church took a good look at their situation. They began bringing the couple food and clothing. They invited them to attend worship services. Bzuneh was not interested. However, his wife, Bililie, was. She began to sober up and consider the story of Christ. The promise of a new life. The offer of a second chance. She believed.

Bzuneh was not so quick. He kept drinking until one night a year later he fell so hard he knocked a dent in his face that remains to this day. Friends found him in a gully and took him to the same church and shared the same Jesus with him. He hasn't touched a drop since.

The problem of poverty continued. The couple owned nothing more than their clothing and mud hut. Enter Meskerem Trango, a World Vision worker. He continued the looking-and-touching ministry. How could he help Bzuneh, a recovering alcoholic, get back on his feet? Jobs in the area were scarce. Besides, who would want to hire the village sot? A gift of cash was not the solution; the couple might drink it away.

Meskerem sat with Bzuneh and explored the options. He finally hit upon a solution. Cow manure. He arranged a loan through the World Vision microfinance department. Bzuneh acquired a cow, built a shed, and began trapping the cow droppings and turning them into methane and fertilizer. Bililie cooked with the gas, and he sold the fertilizer. Within a year Bzuneh had repaid the loan, bought four more cows, built his house, and reclaimed his kids.

"Now I have ten livestock, thirty goats, a TV set, a tape recorder, and a mobile phone. Even my wife has a mobile phone." He smiled. "And I dream of selling grain."

It all began with an honest look and a helping hand. Could this be God's strategy for human hurt? First, kind eyes meet desperate ones. Next, strong hands help weak ones. Then, the miracle of God. We do our small part, he does the big part, and life at the Beautiful Gate begins to be just that.

QUESTIONS FOR REFLECTION AND DISCUSSION

1. "Human hurt is not easy on the eyes." Tell of a time you encountered suffering that was painful to observe. Describe a time you were hurting and someone made you think he or she really *saw* you.

2. What does it communicate to people in need, especially those who are not beautiful, when you look directly at them, in their eyes?

3. Take note of each meaningful touch you find in the following miracles of Jesus: Matthew 9:20–22; Mark 1:40–45; Mark 7:32–35; Luke 8:51–55; Luke 13:11–13; John 9:1–7. Did Jesus need to touch people to heal them? Why do you think some form of touch was part of each healing?

4. Peter and John gave more than the money the crippled beggar asked for in Acts 3. What resources do you have—beyond money—that you could give to people in need?

5. For Peter and John the strategy of kind eyes meeting desperate ones and strong hands helping weak ones unleashed a miracle of God. How could you live out this strategy?

Chapter 16

ISAIAH

"Holy, Holy, Holy, is the LORD of hosts,
The whole earth is full of His glory."

And the foundations of the thresholds trembled at the voice of him who called out, while the temple was filling with smoke. Then I said,

"Woe is me, for I am ruined!
Because I am a man of unclean lips,
And I live among a people of unclean lips;
For my eyes have seen the King, the LORD of hosts."

—ISAIAH 6:2–5 NASB

HOLY DIFFERENT

John Hanning Speke stands on the river edge and stares at the wall of water. He has dedicated the better part of 1858 to getting here. For weeks he and his party slashed through African brush and forded deep rivers. Natives bearing iron-headed spears pursued them. Crocodiles and sterns kept an eye on them. But finally, after miles of jungle marching and grass plodding, they found the falls.

Only a Britisher could so clearly understate the sight. "We were well rewarded," he wrote in his journal.

The roar of the waters, the thousands of passenger fish leaping at the falls with all their might, the Wasoga and Waganda fishermen coming out in boats and taking post on all rocks with rod and hook, hippotami and crocodiles lying sleepily on the water made in all as interesting a picture as one would want to see.[1]

Speke could not leave. He sketched the sight over and over. He dedicated an entire day to simply staring at the majesty of the falls at the upper Nile. Not hard to understand why.

No region of England boasted any such sight. Rarely do eyes fall on a hitherto unseen image. Speke's did. And he was stunned by what he saw.

Fourteen years later, halfway around the globe, Frederick Dellenbaugh was equally impressed. He was only eighteen when he joined Major Powell on his pioneering river voyage through the Grand Canyon. Led by the one-armed Powell, the explorers floated on leaky boats and faced high waters. It's a wonder they survived. It's every bit as much a wonder what they saw. Dellenbaugh described the scene:

My back being towards the fall I could not see it . . . Nearer and nearer came the angry tumult; the Major shouted "Back water!" there was a sudden dropping away of all support; then the mighty wavers [*sic*] smote us. The boat rose to them well, but we were flying at twenty-five miles an hour and at every leap the breakers rolled over us. "Bail!" shouted the Major,—"Bail for your lives!" and we dropped the oars to bail, though bailing was almost useless. . . . The boat rolled and pitched like a ship in a tornado. . . . canopies of foam pour[ed] over gigantic black boulders, first on one side, then on the other. . . . If you will take a watch and count by it ninety seconds, you will probably have about the time we were in this chaos, though it seemed much longer to me. Then we were through.[2]

Young Dellenbaugh knew rapids. Rivers and raging water were not new to him. But something about this river was. The sudden immensity, stark intensity—something stole the oarsman's breath. He knew rapids. But none like this.

Speke, speechless. Dellenbaugh, drenched and awestruck.

And Isaiah, face-first on the temple floor. Arms crossed above his head, muffled voice crying for mercy. Like the explorers, he's just seen the unseen. But unlike the explorers, he's seen more than creation—he's seen the Creator. He's seen God.

Seven and one-half centuries before Christ, Isaiah was ancient Israel's version of a Senate chaplain or court priest. His family, aristocratic. His Hebrew, impeccable. Polished, professional, and successful. But the day he saw God only one response seemed appropriate: "Woe is me, for I am ruined." What caused such a confession? What stirred such a reply? The answer is found in the thrice-repeated words of the seraphim: "Holy, holy, holy."

Seraphim stood above Him, each having six wings: with two he covered his face, and with two he covered his feet, and with two he flew. And one called out to another and said,

"Holy, Holy, Holy, is the LORD of hosts,
The whole earth is full of His glory."

152

And the foundations of the thresholds trembled at the voice of him
who called out, while the temple was filling with smoke. Then I said,

"Woe is me, for I am ruined!
Because I am a man of unclean lips,
And I live among a people of unclean lips;
For my eyes have seen the King, the LORD of hosts." (Isa. 6:2–5 NASB)

On the one occasion seraphim appear in Scripture, they endlessly
trilogize the same word.

"Holy, holy, holy is the LORD Almighty" (NIV). Repetition, in Hebrew,
performs the work of our highlighter. A tool of emphasis. God, proclaims the six-winged angels, is not holy. He is not holy, holy. He is holy,
holy, holy.

What other attribute receives such enforcement? No verse describes
God as "wise, wise, wise" or "strong, strong, strong." Only as "holy,
holy, holy." God's holiness commands headline attention. The adjec-
tive qualifies his name more than all other combined.[3] The first and
final songs of the Bible magnify the holiness of God. Having crossed
the Red Sea, Moses and the Israelites sang, "Who among the gods is like
you, O LORD? Who is like you—majestic in holiness, awesome in glory,
working wonders?" (Ex. 15:11 NIV). In Revelation those who had been
victorious over the beast sang, "Who will not fear you, O Lord, and
bring glory to your name? For you alone are holy" (15:4 NIV).

The Hebrew word for *holy* is *qadosh*, which means cut off or separate.
Holiness, then, speaks of the "otherness" of God. His total uniqueness.
Everything about God is different from the world he has made.

What you are to a paper airplane, God is to you. Take a sheet of
paper and make one. Contrast yourself with your creation. Challenge it
to a spelling contest. Who will win?

Dare it to race you around the block. Who is faster? Invite the airplane
to a game of one-on-one basketball. Will you not dominate the court?

And well you should. The thing has no brain waves, no pulse. It exists only because you formed it and flies only when someone throws it. Multiply the contrasts between you and the paper airplane by infinity, and you will begin to catch a glimpse of the disparity between God and us.

To what can we compare God? "Who in the skies is comparable to the LORD? Who among the sons of the mighty is like the LORD?"(Ps. 89:6 NASB). "To whom then will you liken God? Or what likeness will you compare with Him?" (Isa. 40:18 NASB). Even God asks, "To whom will you compare me? Who is my equal?" (Isa. 40:25 NLT).

As if his question needed an answer, he gives one:

> I am God—I alone! I am God, and there is no one else like me. Only I can tell you what is going to happen even before it happens. Everything I plan will come to pass, for I do whatever I wish. I will call a swift bird of prey from the east—a leader from a distant land who will come and do my bidding. I have said I would do it, and I will. (Isa. 46:9–11 NLT)

Any pursuit of God's counterpart is vain. Any search for godlike person or position on earth is futile. No one and nothing compares with him. No one advises him. No one helps him. It is he who "executes judgment, putting down one and lifting up another" (Ps. 75:7 ESV).

You and I may have power. But God *is* power. We may be a lightning bug, but he is lightning itself. "Wisdom and power are his" (Dan. 2:20 NIV).

Consider the universe around us. Unlike the potter who takes something and reshapes it, God took nothing and created something. God created everything that exists by divine fiat *ex nihilo* (out of nothing). He did not rely on material that was preexistent or coeternal. Prior to creation the universe was not a dark space. The universe did not exist.

God even created the darkness. "I am the one who creates the light and makes the darkness" (Isa. 45:7 NLT). John proclaimed, "You created everything, and it is for your pleasure that they exist and were created" (Rev. 4:11 NLT).

Trace the universe back to God's power, and follow his power upstream to his wisdom. God's omniscience governs his omnipotence. Infinite knowledge rules infinite strength. "He is wise in heart, and mighty in strength" (Job 9:4 KJV). "He is mighty in strength and wisdom" (Job 36:5 KJV).

His power is not capricious or careless. Quite the contrary, his wisdom manages and equals his strength. Paul announced, "Oh, the depth of the riches of the wisdom and knowledge of God! How unsearchable his judgments, and his paths beyond tracing out" (Rom. 11:33 NIV).

His knowledge about you is as complete as his knowledge about the universe. "Even before a word is on my tongue, behold, O LORD, you know it altogether. . . . Your eyes saw my unformed substance; in your book were written, every one of them, the days that were formed for me, when as yet there was none of them" (Ps. 139:4, 16 ESV).

The veils that block your vision and mine do not block God's. Unspoken words are as if uttered. Unrevealed thoughts are as if proclaimed. Unoccurred moments are as if they were history. He knows the future, the past, the hidden, and the untold. Nothing is concealed from God. He is all-powerful, all-knowing, and all-present.

King David marveled, "Where can I go from Your Spirit? Or where can I flee from Your presence?" (Ps. 139:7 NASB). God reminds us, "I am everywhere—both near and far, in heaven and on earth" (Jer. 23:23–24 CEV).

See the "holy otherness" of God? In Isaiah's encounter, those who see him most clearly regard him most highly. He is so holy that sinless seraphim cannot bear to look at him!

They cover their faces with their wings. They also, oddly, cover their feet. Why? In Hebrew the word *feet* and the word for *genitalia* are the same.[4] Forgive the thought, but the confession of the angels is that they are absolutely impotent in the presence of God.

Isaiah could relate. When he sees the holiness of God, Isaiah does not boast or swagger. He takes no notes, plans no sermon series, launches no seminar tours. Instead, he falls on his face and begs for mercy. "Woe is me, for I am ruined! Because I am a man of unclean lips, and I live among people of unclean lips; for my eyes have seen the King, the Lord of hosts" (Isa. 6:5 NASB).

The God-given vision was not about Isaiah but about God and his glory. Isaiah gets the point. "It's not about me. It's all about him." He finds humility, not through seeking it, but through seeking him. One glimpse and the prophet claims citizenship among the infected and diseased—the "unclean," a term used to describe those with leprosy. God's holiness silences human boasting.

And God's mercy makes us holy. Look what happens next.

> Then one of the seraphim flew to me with a burning coal in his hand, which he had taken from the altar with tongs. He touched my mouth with it and said, "Behold, this has touched your lips; and your iniquity is taken away and your sin is forgiven." (vv. 6–7 NASB)

Isaiah makes no request. He asks for no grace. Indeed, he likely assumed mercy was impossible. But God, who is quick to pardon and full of mercy, purges Isaiah of his sin and redirects his life.

God solicits a spokesman. "Whom shall I send, and who will go for Us?" (v. 8 NASB)

Isaiah's heart and hand shoot skyward. "Here am I. Send me!" (v. 8 NASB). A glimpse of God's holiness and Isaiah had to speak. As if he'd found the source of the river, ridden the rage of the canyon. As if he'd seen what Moses had seen—God himself. Albeit a glimpse, but a God-glimpse nonetheless.

And he was different as a result.

Holy different.

QUESTIONS FOR REFLECTION AND DISCUSSION

1. What does "holiness" mean to you? How would you describe it to someone who knows nothing about the Bible?
2. How does God's holiness silence human boasting?
3. When was the last time you experienced God's quick pardon and fullness of mercy? Describe what happened.
4. Read Isaiah 6:1–8. How does Isaiah react to this revelation of God's glory (v. 5)? How do you think you would have reacted? Explain.
5. What resulted from Isaiah's cleansing (v. 8)? How do you think God wants to use Isaiah's experience in your own life?

Chapter 17

THE
GADARENE
DEMONIAC

When He got out of the boat, immediately a man from the tombs with an unclean spirit met Him, and he had his dwelling among the tombs. And no one was able to bind him anymore, even with a chain; because he had often been bound with shackles and chains, and the chains had been torn apart by him and the shackles broken in pieces, and no one was strong enough to subdue him. Constantly, night and day, he was screaming among the tombs and in the mountains, and gashing himself with stones.

—MARK 5:2–5 NASB

Getting the Hell Out

Wiry, clumpy hair. A beard to the chest, ribboned with blood. Furtive eyes, darting in all directions, refusing to fix. Naked. No sandals to protect feet from the rocks of the ground or clothing to protect skin from the rocks of his hand. He beats himself with stones. Bruises blotch his skin like ink stains. Open sores and gashes attract flies.

His home is a limestone mausoleum, a graveyard of Galilean shoreline caves cut out of the cliffs. Apparently he feels more secure among the dead than the living.

Which pleases the living. He baffles them. See the cracked shackles on his legs and broken chains on his wrists? They can't control the guy. Nothing holds him. How do you manage chaos? Travelers skirt the area out of fear (Matt. 8:28). The villagers were left with a problem, and we are left with a picture—a picture of the work of Satan.

How else do we explain our bizarre behavior? The violent rages of a father. The secret binges of a mother. The sudden rebellion of a teenager. Maxed-out credit cards, Internet pornography. Satan does not sit still. A glimpse of the wild man reveals Satan's goals for you and me.

Self-imposed pain. The demoniac used rocks. We are more sophisticated; we use drugs, sex, work, violence, and food. (Hell makes us hurt ourselves.)

Obsession with death and darkness. Even unchained, the wild man loitered among the dead. Evil feels at home there. Communing with the deceased, sacrificing the living, a morbid fascination with death and dying—this is not the work of God.

Endless restlessness. The man on the eastern shore screamed day and night (Mark 5:5). Satan begets raging frenzy. "The evil spirit . . . wanders . . ." Jesus says, "looking for rest" (Matt. 12:43 PHILLIPS).

Isolation. The man is all alone in his suffering. Such is Satan's plan. "The devil prowls around like a roaring lion, seeking some *one* to devour" (1 Peter 5:8 RSV; emphasis added). Fellowship foils his work.

And Jesus?

Jesus wrecks his work. Christ steps out of the boat with both pistols blasting. "Come out of the man, unclean spirit!" (Mark 5:8 NKJV).

No chitchat. No niceties. No salutations. Demons deserve no tolerance. They throw themselves at the feet and mercy of Christ. The leader of the horde begs for the others:

> "What have you to do with me, Jesus, Son of the Most High God? I adjure you by God, do not torment me." . . . Jesus asked him, "What is your name?" He replied, "My name is Legion; for we are many." He begged him earnestly not to send them out of the country. (vv. 7, 9–10 NRSV)

Legion is a Roman military term. A Roman legion involved six thousand soldiers. To envision that many demons inhabiting this man is frightening but not unrealistic. What bats are to a cave, demons are to hell—too many to number.

The demons are not only numerous, they are equipped. A legion is a battalion in arms. Satan and his friends come to fight. Hence, we are urged to "take up the full armor of God, so that you will be able to resist in the evil day, and having done everything, to stand firm" (Eph. 6:13 NASB).

Well, we should, for they are organized. "We are fighting against forces and authorities and against rulers of darkness and powers in the spiritual world" (Eph. 6:12 CEV). Jesus spoke of the "gates of hell" (Matt. 16:18 KJV), a phrase that suggests the "council of hell." Our enemy has a complex and conniving spiritual army. Dismiss any image of a red-suited Satan with pitchfork and pointy tail. The devil is a strong devil.

But, and this is the point of the passage, in God's presence, the devil is a wimp. Satan is to God what a mosquito is to an atomic bomb.

Now a large herd of swine was feeding there near the mountains. So all the demons begged Him, saying, "Send us to the swine, that we may enter them." And at once Jesus gave them permission. Then the unclean spirits went out and entered the swine (there were about two thousand); and the herd ran violently down the steep place into the sea, and drowned in the sea. (Mark 5:11–13 NKJV)

How hell's court cowers in Christ's presence! Demons bow before him, solicit him, and obey him. They can't even lease a pig without his permission. Then how do we explain Satan's influence?

Natalie[1] must have asked that question a thousand times. In the list of characters for a modern-day Gerasenes story, her name is near the top. She was raised in a tormented world.

The community suspected nothing. Her parents cast a friendly facade. Each Sunday they paraded Natalie and her sisters down the church aisle. Her father served as an elder. Her mom played the organ. The congregation respected them. Natalie despised them. To this day she refuses to call her parents "Mom" and "Dad." A "warlock" and "witch" don't deserve the distinction.

When she was six months old, they sexually sacrificed Natalie on hell's altar, tagging her as a sex object to be exploited by men in any place, anytime. Cultists bipolarized her world: dressing her in white for Sunday service and, hours later, stripping her at the coven. If she didn't scream or vomit during the attack, Natalie was rewarded with an ice cream cone. Only by "crawling down deep" inside herself could she survive.

Natalie miraculously escaped the cult but not the memories. Well into her adult years, she wore six pairs of underpants as a wall of protection. Dresses created vulnerability; she avoided them. She hated being a woman; she hated seeing men; she hated being alive. Only God could know the legion of terrors that dogged her. But God did know.

Hidden within the swampland of her soul was an untouched island. Small but safe. Built, she believes, by her heavenly Father during the hours the little girl sat on a church pew. Words of his love, hymns of his mercy—they left their mark. She learned to retreat to this island and pray. God heard her prayers. Counselors came. Hope began to off-set horror. Her faith increasingly outweighed her fears. The healing process was lengthy and tedious but victorious, culminating in her marriage to a godly man.[2]

Her deliverance didn't include cliffs and pigs, but, make no mistake, she was delivered. And we are reminded. Satan can disturb us, but he cannot defeat us. The head of the serpent is crushed.

I saw a literal picture of this in a prairie ditch. A petroleum company was hiring strong backs and weak minds to lay a pipeline. Since I qualified, much of a high school summer was spent shoveling in a shoulder-high, multimile West Texas trough. A large digging machine trenched ahead of us. We followed, scooping out the excess dirt and rocks.

One afternoon the machine dislodged more than dirt. "Snake!" shouted the foreman. We popped out of that hole faster than a jack-in-the-box and looked down at the rattlesnake nest. Big momma hissed, and her little kids squirmed. Reentering the trench was not an option. One worker launched his shovel and beheaded the rattler. We stood on the higher ground and watched as she—now headless—writhed and twisted in the soft dirt below. Though defanged, the snake still spooked us.

That scene in the West Texas summer is a parable of where we are in life. Is the devil not a snake? John calls him "that old snake who is the devil" (Rev. 20:2).

Has he not been decapitated? Not with a shovel, but with a cross. "God disarmed the evil rulers and authorities. He shamed them publicly by his victory over them on the cross of Christ" (Col. 2:15 NLT).

So how does that leave us? *Confident*. The punch line of the pas-sage is Jesus' power over Satan. One word from Christ, and the demons are swimming with the swine and the wild man is "clothed and in his right mind" (Mark 5:15 NASB). Just one command! No séance needed. No hocus-pocus. No chants were heard or candles lit. Hell is an anthill against heaven's steamroller. Jesus "commands . . . evil spirits, and they obey him" (Mark 1:27). The snake in the ditch and Lucifer in the pit—both have met their match.

And yet, both stir up dust long after their defeat. For that reason, though confident, we are still *careful*. For a toothless ol' varmint, Satan sure has some bite! He spooks our work, disrupts our activities, and leaves us thinking twice about where we step. Which we need to do. "Be self-controlled and alert. Your enemy the devil prowls around like a roaring lion looking for someone to devour" (1 Peter 5:8 NIV). Alertness is needed. Panic is not. The serpent still wiggles and intimidates, but he has no poison. He is defeated, and he knows it! "He knows his time is short" (Rev. 12:12 CEV).

"Greater is He who is in you than he who is in the world" (1 John 4:4 NASB). Believe it. Trust the work of your Savior. "Resist the devil and he will flee from you" (James 4:7 NASB). In the meantime, the best he can do is squirm.

QUESTIONS FOR REFLECTION AND DISCUSSION

1. Max says, "A glimpse of the wild man reveals Satan's goals for you and me. *Self-imposed pain.* The demoniac used rocks. We are more sophisticated; we use drugs, sex, work, violence, and food." How have you seen people around you suffer from self-imposed pain? In what way(s) has hell made you hurt yourself?

2. Read Mark 5:1–20. Why could Christ control the demons with a single command? What does it mean for you that Christ has such power over hell?

3. Why do you think the demon-possessed man came out to meet Jesus when the Lord got out of the boat (Mark 5:2)? Why wouldn't he just run away?

4. What did the cured man request of Jesus (Mark 5:18)? What answer did Jesus give (v. 19)? Why do you think he gave this answer?

5. Read 1 Peter 5:8–10. How do you steady yourself so that you stand "strong in your faith"? Why does it help to remember that you are not alone in suffering and temptation (v. 9)? From where does all spiritual strength ultimately come (v. 10)?

❦

Chapter 18

THE LEPER
JESUS HEALED

Since you have been chosen by God who has given you this new kind of life, and because of his deep love and concern for you, you should practice tenderhearted mercy and kindness to others.

—Colossians 3:12 TLB

A Compassionate Touch

May I ask you to look at your hand for a moment? Look at the back, then the palm. Reacquaint yourself with your fingers. Run a thumb over your knuckles.

What if someone were to film a documentary about your hands? What if a producer were to tell your story based on the life of your hands? What would we see? As with all of us, the film would begin with an infant's fist, then a close-up of a tiny hand wrapped around mommy's finger. Then what? Holding on to a chair as you learned to walk? Handling a spoon as you learned to eat?

We aren't too long into the feature before we see your hand being affectionate, stroking daddy's face or petting a puppy. Nor is it too long before we see your hand acting aggressively: pushing big brother or yanking back a toy. All of us learned early that the hand is suited for more than survival—it's a tool of emotional expression. The same hand can help or hurt, extend or clench, lift someone up or shove someone down.

Were you to show the documentary to your friends, you'd be proud of certain moments: your hand extending with a gift, placing a ring on another's finger, doctoring a wound, preparing a meal, or folding in prayer. And then there are other scenes. Shots of accusing fingers, abusive fists. Hands taking more often than giving, demanding instead of offering, wounding rather than loving. Oh, the power of our hands. Leave them unmanaged and they become weapons: clawing for power, strangling for survival, seducing for pleasure. But manage them and our hands become instruments of grace—not just tools in the hands of God, but *God's very hands*. Surrender them and these five-fingered append-ages become the hands of heaven.

That's what Jesus did. Our Savior completely surrendered his hands to God. The documentary of his hands has no scenes of greedy grabbing or unfounded finger pointing. It does, however, have one scene after another of people longing for his compassionate touch: parents carrying their children, the poor bringing their fears, the sinful shouldering their sorrow. And each who came was touched. And each one touched was changed. But none was touched or changed more than the unnamed leper of Matthew 8.

> When Jesus came down from the hill, great crowds followed him. Then a man with a skin disease came to Jesus. The man bowed down before him and said, "Lord, you can heal me if you will."
>
> Jesus reached out his hand and touched the man and said, "I will. Be healed!" And immediately the man was healed from his disease. Then Jesus said to him, "Don't tell anyone about this. But go and show yourself to the priest and offer the gift Moses commanded for people who are made well. This will show the people what I have done." (vv. 1–4)

Mark and Luke chose to tell this same story. But with apologies to all three writers, I must say none tell enough. Oh, we know the man's disease and his decision, but as to the rest? We are left with questions. The authors offer no name, no history, no description.

Sometimes my curiosity gets the best of me, and I wonder out loud. That's what I'm about to do here—wonder out loud about the man who felt Jesus' compassionate touch. He makes one appearance, has one request, and receives one touch. But that one touch changed his life forever. And I wonder if his story went something like this:

For five years no one touched me. No one. Not one person. Not my wife. Not my child. Not my friends. No one touched me. They saw me. They spoke to me. I sensed love in their voices. I saw concern in their eyes. But I didn't feel their touch. There was no touch. Not once. No one touched me.

What is common to you, I coveted. Handshakes. Warm embraces. A tap on the shoulder to get my attention. A kiss on the lips to steal a heart. Such moments were taken from my world. No one touched me. No one bumped into me. What I would have given to be bumped into, to be caught in a crowd, for my shoulder to brush against another's. But for five years it has not happened. How could it? I was not allowed on the streets. Even the rabbis kept their distance from me. I was not permitted in my synagogue. Not even welcome in my own house.

I was untouchable. I was a leper. And no one touched me. Until today.

I wonder about this man because in New Testament times leprosy was the most dreaded disease. The condition rendered the body a mass of ulcers and decay. Fingers would curl and gnarl. Blotches of skin would discolor and stink. Certain types of leprosy would numb nerve endings, leading to a loss of fingers, toes, even a whole foot or hand. Leprosy was death by inches.

The social consequences were as severe as the physical. Considered contagious, the leper was quarantined, banished to a leper colony.

In Scripture the leper is symbolic of the ultimate outcast: infected by a condition he did not seek, rejected by those he knew, avoided by people he did not know, condemned to a future he could not bear. And in the memory of each outcast must have been the day he was forced to face the truth: life would never be the same.

One year during harvest my grip on the scythe seemed weak. The tips of my fingers numbed. First one finger, then another. Within a short time I could grip the tool but scarcely feel it. By the end of the season, I felt nothing at all. The hand grasping the handle might as well have belonged to someone else—the feeling was gone. I said nothing to my wife, but I know she suspected something. How could she not? I carried my hand against my body like a wounded bird.

One afternoon I plunged my hands into a basin of water intending to wash my face. The water reddened. My finger was bleeding, bleeding freely. I didn't even know I was wounded. How did I cut myself? On a knife? Did my hand slide across the sharp edge of metal? It must have, but I didn't feel anything.

"It's on your clothes too," my wife said softly. She was behind me. Before looking at her, I looked down at the crimson spots on my robe. For the longest

time I stood over the basin, staring at my hand. Somehow I knew my life was being forever altered.

"Shall I go with you to tell the priest?" she asked.

"No," I sighed, "I'll go alone."

I turned and looked into her moist eyes. Standing next to her was our three-year-old daughter. Squatting, I gazed into her face and stroked her cheek, saying nothing. What could I say? I stood and looked again at my wife. She touched my shoulder, and with my good hand, I touched hers. It would be our final touch.

Five years have passed, and no one has touched me since, until today.

The priest didn't touch me. He looked at my hand, now wrapped in a rag. He looked at my face, now shadowed in sorrow. I've never faulted him for what he said. He was only doing as he was instructed. He covered his mouth and extended his hand, palm forward. "You are unclean," he told me. With one pronouncement I lost my family, my farm, my future, my friends.

My wife met me at the city gates with a sack of clothing and bread and coins. She didn't speak. By now friends had gathered. What I saw in their eyes was a precursor to what I've seen in every eye since: fearful pity. As I stepped out, they stepped back. Their horror of my disease was greater than their concern for my heart—so they, and everyone else I have seen since, stepped back.

The banishing of a leper seems harsh, unnecessary. The Ancient East hasn't been the only culture to isolate their wounded, however. We may not build colonies or cover our mouths in their presence, but we certainly build walls and duck our eyes. And a person needn't have leprosy to feel quarantined.

One of my sadder memories involves my fourth-grade friend Jerry.[1] He and a half dozen of us were an ever-present, inseparable fixture on the playground. One day I called his house to see if we could play. The phone was answered by a cursing, drunken voice telling me Jerry could not come over that day or any day. I told my friends what had happened. One of them explained that Jerry's father was an alcoholic. I don't know if I knew what the word meant, but I learned quickly. Jerry, the second baseman; Jerry, the kid with the red bike; Jerry, my friend on the corner was now "Jerry, the son of a drunk." Kids can be hard, and for some reason we were hard on Jerry. He was infected. Like the leper, he suffered from a condition he didn't create. Like the leper, he was put outside the village.

The divorced know this feeling. So do the handicapped. The unemployed have felt it, as have the less educated. Some shun unmarried moms. We keep our distance from the depressed and avoid the terminally ill. We have neighborhoods for immigrants, convalescent homes for the elderly, schools for the simple, centers for the addicted, and prisons for the criminals.

The rest simply try to get away from it all. Only God knows how many Jerrys are in voluntary exile—individuals living quiet, lonely lives infected by their fear of rejection and their memories of the last time they tried. They choose not to be touched at all rather than risk being hurt again.

Oh, how I repulsed those who saw me. Five years of leprosy had left my hands gnarled. Tips of my fingers were missing as were portions of an ear and my nose. At the sight of me, fathers grabbed their children. Mothers covered their faces. Children pointed and stared.

The rags on my body couldn't hide my sores. Nor could the wrap on my face hide the rage in my eyes. I didn't even try to hide it. How many nights did I shake my crippled fist at the silent sky? "What did I do to deserve this?" But never a reply.

Some think I sinned. Some think my parents sinned. I don't know. All I know is that I grew so tired of it all: sleeping in the colony, smelling the stench. I grew so tired of the damnable bell I was required to wear around my neck to warn people of my presence. As if I needed it. One glance and the announcements began, "Unclean! Unclean! Unclean!"

Several weeks ago I dared walk the road to my village. I had no intent of entering. Heaven knows I only wanted to look again upon my fields. Gaze again upon my home. And see, perchance, the face of my wife. I did not see her. But I saw some children playing in a pasture. I hid behind a tree and watched them scamper and run. Their faces were so joyful and their laughter so contagious that for a moment, for just a moment, I was no longer a leper. I was a farmer. I was a father. I was a man.

Infused with their happiness, I stepped out from behind the tree, straightened my back, breathed deeply . . . and they saw me. Before I could retreat, they saw me. And they screamed. And they scattered. One lingered, though, behind the others. One paused and looked in my direction. I don't know, and I can't say for sure, but I think, I really think, she was my daughter. And I don't know, I really can't say for sure. But I think she was looking for her father.

That look is what made me take the step I took today. Of course it was reckless. Of course it was risky. But what did I have to lose? He calls himself God's Son. Either he will hear my complaint and kill me or accept my demands and heal me. Those were my thoughts. I came to him as a defiant man. Moved not by faith but by a desperate anger. God had wrought this calamity on my body, and he would either fix it or end it.

But then I saw him, and when I saw him, I was changed. You must remember, I'm a farmer, not a poet, so I cannot find the words to describe what I saw. All I can say is that the Judean mornings are sometimes so fresh and the sunrises so glorious that to look at them is to forget the heat of the day before and the hurt of times past. When I looked at his face, I saw a Judean morning.

Before he spoke, I knew he cared. Somehow I knew he hated this disease as much as, no—more—than I hate it. My rage became trust, and my anger became hope.

From behind a rock, I watched him descend a hill. Throngs of people followed him. I waited until he was only paces from me, then I stepped out.

"Master!"

He stopped and looked in my direction, as did dozens of others. A flood of fear swept across the crowd. Arms flew in front of faces. Children ducked behind parents. "Unclean!" someone shouted. Again, I don't blame them. I was a huddled mass of death. But I scarcely heard them. I scarcely saw them. Their panic I'd seen a thousand times. His compassion, however, I'd never beheld. Everyone stepped back except him. He stepped toward me. Toward me.

Five years ago my wife had stepped toward me. She was the last to do so. Now he did. I did not move. I just spoke. "Lord, you can heal me if you will."

Had he healed me with a word, I would have been thrilled. Had he cured me with a prayer, I would have rejoiced. But he wasn't satisfied with speaking to me. He drew near me. He touched me. Five years ago my wife had touched me. No one had touched me since. Until today.

"I will." His words were as tender as his touch. "Be healed!"

Energy flooded my body like water through a furrowed field. In an instant, in a moment, I felt warmth where there had been numbness. I felt strength where there had been atrophy. My back straightened, and my head lifted. Where I had been eye level with his belt, I now stood eye level with his face. His smiling face.

He cupped his hands on my cheeks and drew me so near I could feel the warmth of his breath and see the wetness in his eyes. "Don't tell anyone about this. But go and show yourself to the priest and offer the gift Moses commanded for people who are made well. This will show the people what I have done."

And so that is where I am going. I will show myself to my priest and embrace him. I will show myself to my wife, and I will embrace her. I will pick up my daughter, and I will embrace her. And I will never forget the one who dared to touch me. He could have healed me with a word. But he wanted to do more than heal me. He wanted to honor me, to validate me, to christen me. Imagine that . . . unworthy of the touch of a man, yet worthy of the touch of God.

The touch did not heal the disease, you know. Matthew is careful to mention that it was the pronouncement and not the touch of Christ that cured the condition. "Jesus reached out his hand and touched the man and said, 'I will. Be healed!' And immediately the man was healed from his disease" (Matt. 8:3).

The infection was banished by a word from Jesus.

The loneliness, however, was treated by a touch from Jesus.

Oh, the power of a godly touch. Haven't you known it? The doctor who treated you, or the teacher who dried your tears? Was there a hand holding yours at a funeral? Another on your shoulder during a trial? A handshake of welcome at a new job? A pastoral prayer for healing? Haven't we known the power of a godly touch?

Can't we offer the same?

Many of you already do. Some of you have the master touch of the

Physician himself. You use your hands to pray over the sick and minister to the weak. If you aren't touching them personally, your hands are writing letters, dialing phones, baking pies. You have learned the power of a touch.

But others of us tend to forget. Our hearts are good; it's just that our memories are bad. We forget how significant one touch can be. We fear saying the wrong thing or using the wrong tone or acting the wrong way. So rather than do it incorrectly, we do nothing at all.

Aren't we glad Jesus didn't make the same mistake? If your fear of doing the wrong thing prevents you from doing anything, keep in mind the perspective of the lepers of the world. They aren't picky. They aren't finicky. They're just lonely. They are yearning for a godly touch.

Jesus touched the untouchables of the world. Will you do the same?

QUESTIONS FOR REFLECTION AND DISCUSSION

1. Have you ever "quarantined" someone from your life? If so, what was the situation? Why did you make the exclusion? What would cause you to include him or her again?

2. Though Jesus' words cured the leper's disease, Max points out that only Christ's loving touch banished the man's loneliness. Describe a time in your life when no words came, but a touch said it all.

3. Read again the story of the cleansed leper from Matthew 8:1–4. Why do you think Jesus thought it was important to physically touch the man? Would the story have been diminished without the touch? Explain.

4. Read Mark 1:40–45. The cleansed leper, though having been warned not to tell the story to anyone, instead went out and began to talk freely. Would you have been able to keep quiet if such a marvelous thing had happened to you? Explain.

5. Think of someone who has a compassionate spirit. How is this spirit expressed through his or her actions, speech, and demeanor? With the Lord's help, how can you work at better showing compassion?

Chapter 19

❧

MEPHIBOSHETH

David asked, "Is anyone still left in Saul's family? I want to show kindness to that person for Jonathan's sake!"

Now there was a servant named Ziba from Saul's family. So David's servants called Ziba to him. King David said to him, "Are you Ziba?"

He answered, "Yes, I am your servant."

The king asked, "Is anyone left in Saul's family? I want to show God's kindness to that person."

Ziba answered the king, "Jonathan has a son still living who is crippled in both feet."

The king asked Ziba, "Where is this son?"

Ziba answered, "He is at the house of Makir son of Ammiel in Lo Debar."

Then King David had servants bring Jonathan's son from the house of Makir son of Ammiel in Lo Debar. Mephibosheth, Jonathan's son, came before David and bowed facedown on the floor.

David said, "Mephibosheth!"

Mephibosheth said, "I am your servant."

David said to him, "Don't be afraid. I will be kind to you for your father Jonathan's sake. I will give you back all the land of your grandfather Saul, and you will always eat at my table."

Mephibosheth bowed to David again and said, "You are being very kind to me, your servant! And I am no better than a dead dog!"

Then King David called Saul's servant Ziba. David said to him, "I have given your master's grandson everything that belonged to Saul and his family. You, your sons, and your servants will farm the land and harvest the crops. Then your family will have food to eat. But Mephibosheth, your master's grandson, will always eat at my table."

(Now Ziba had fifteen sons and twenty servants.) Ziba said to King David, "I, your servant, will do everything my master, the king, commands me."

So Mephibosheth ate at David's table as if he were one of the king's sons. Mephibosheth had a young son named Mica. Everyone in Ziba's family became Mephibosheth's servants. Mephibosheth lived in Jerusalem, because he always ate at the king's table. And he was crippled in both feet.

—2 SAMUEL 9:1–13

WHEN GRACE GOES DEEP

The prodigal son trudges up the path. His pig stink makes pass-ersby walk wide circles around him, but he doesn't notice. With eyes on the ground, he rehearses his speech: "Father"—his voice barely audible—"I have sinned against heaven and against you. I'm not worthy to be called your son." He rehashes the phrases, wondering if he should say more, say less, or make a U-turn to the barnyard. After all, he cashed in the trust fund and trashed the family name. Over the last year, he'd awakened with more parched throats, headaches, women, and tattoos than a rock star. How could his father forgive him? *Maybe I could offer to pay off the credit cards.* He's so focused on penance planning that he fails to hear the sound of his father . . . running!

The dad embraces the mud-layered boy as if he were a returning war hero. He commands the servants to bring a robe, ring, and sandals, as if to say, "No boy of mine is going to look like a pigpen peasant. Fire up the grill. Bring on the drinks. It's time for a party!"

Big brother meanwhile stands on the porch and sulks. "No one ever gave me a party," he mumbles, arms crossed.

The father tries to explain, but the jealous son won't listen. He huffs and shrugs and grumbles something about cheap grace, saddles his high horse, and rides off. But you knew that. You've read the parable of the gracious father and the hostile brother (Luke 15:11–32).

But have you heard what happened next? Have you read the second chapter? It's a page-turner. The older brother resolves to rain on the for-giveness parade. *If Dad won't exact justice on the boy, I will.*

"Nice robe there, little brother," he tells him one day. "Better keep it clean. One spot and Dad will send you to the cleaners with it."

The younger brother waves him away, but the next time he sees his father, he quickly checks his robe for stains.

A few days later big brother warns about the ring. "Quite a piece of jewelry Dad gave you. He prefers that you wear it on the thumb."

"The thumb? He didn't tell me that."

"Some things we're just supposed to know."

"But it won't fit my thumb."

"What's your goal—pleasing our father or your own personal comfort?" the spirituality monitor gibes, walking away.

Big brother isn't finished. With the pleasantness of a dyspeptic IRS auditor, he taunts, "If Dad sees you with loose laces, he'll take the sandals back."

"He will not. They were a gift. He wouldn't . . . would he?" The ex-prodigal then leans over to snug the strings. As he does, he spots a smudge on his robe. Trying to rub it off, he realizes the ring is on a finger, not his thumb. That's when he hears his father's voice. "Hello, son."

There the boy sits, wearing a spotted robe, loose laces, and a misplaced ring. Overcome with fear, he reacts with a "Sorry, Dad" and turns and runs.

Too many tasks. Keeping the robe spotless, the ring positioned, the sandals snug—who could meet such standards? Gift preservation begins to wear on the young man. He avoids the father he feels he can't please. He quits wearing the gifts he can't maintain. And he even begins longing for the simpler days of the pigpen. "No one hounded me there."

That's the rest of the story. Wondering where I found it? On page 1,892 of my Bible, in the book of Galatians. Thanks to some legalistic big brothers, Paul's readers had gone from grace receiving to law keeping. Their Christian life had taken on the joy level of an upper G.I. endoscopy. Paul was puzzled.

> I am shocked that you are turning away so soon from God, who in his love and mercy called you to share the eternal life he gives through Christ. You are already following a different way that pretends to be the Good News but is not the Good News at all. You are being fooled by those who twist and change the truth concerning Christ. . . .

And yet we Jewish Christians know that we become right with
God, not by doing what the law commands, but by faith in Jesus Christ.
So we have believed in Christ Jesus, that we might be accepted by God
because of our faith in Christ—and not because we have obeyed the law.
For no one will ever be saved by obeying the law. (Gal. 1:6–7; 2:16 NLT)

Joy snatchers infiltrated the Roman church as well. Paul had to
remind them, "But people are declared righteous because of their faith,
not because of their work" (Rom. 4:5 NLT).

Philippian Christians heard the same foolishness. Big brothers
weren't telling them to wear a ring on their thumb, but they were insist-
ing "you must be circumcised to be saved" (Phil. 3:2 NLT).

Even the Jerusalem church, the flagship congregation, heard the
solemn monotones of the Quality Control Board. Non-Jewish believers were being told, "You cannot be saved if you are not circumcised as
Moses taught us" (Acts 15:1).

The churches suffered from the same malady: grace blockage. The
Father might let you in the gate, but you have to earn your place at the
table. God makes the down payment on your redemption, but you pay
the monthly installments. Heaven gives the boat, but you have to row it
if you ever want to see the other shore.

Grace blockage. Taste, but don't drink. Wet your lips, but never
slake your thirst. Can you imagine such instruction over a fountain?
"No swallowing, please. Fill your mouth but not your belly."

Absurd. What good is water if you can't drink it? And what good is
grace if you don't let it go deep?

Do you? What image best describes your heart? A water-drenched
kid dancing in front of an open fire hydrant? Or a bristled desert tumble-
weed? Here is how you know. One question. Does God's grace *define*
you? Deeply flowing grace clarifies, once and for all, who we are.

But God is so rich in mercy, and he loved us so very much, that even
while we were dead because of our sins, he gave us life when he raised

Christ from the dead. (It is only by God's special favor that you have been saved!) For he raised us from the dead along with Christ, and we are seated with him in the heavenly realms—all because we are one with Christ Jesus. And so God can always point to us as examples of the incredible wealth of his favor and kindness toward us, as shown in all he has done for us through Christ Jesus.

God saved you by his special favor when you believed. And you can't take credit for this; it is a gift from God. Salvation is not a reward for the good things we have done, so none of us can boast about it. (Eph. 2:4–9 NLT)

Look how grace defines us. We are

- spiritually alive: "he gave us life" (v. 5 NLT);
- heavenly positioned: "seated with him in the heavenly realms" (v. 6 NLT);
- connected to God: "one with Christ Jesus" (v. 6 NLT);
- billboards of mercy: "examples of the incredible wealth of his favor and kindness toward us" (v. 7 NLT);
- honored children: "God saved you by his special favor" (v. 8 NLT).

Grace defines you. As grace sinks in, earthly labels fade. Society labels you like a can on an assembly line. Stupid. Unproductive. Slow learner. Fast talker. Quitter. Cheapskate. But as grace infiltrates, criticism disintegrates. You know you aren't who they say you are. You are who God says you are. Spiritually alive. Heavenly positioned. Connected to the Father. A billboard of mercy. An honored child.

Of course, not all labels are negative. Some people regard you as handsome, clever, successful, or efficient. But even a White House office doesn't compare with being "seated with him in the heavenly realms." Grace creates the Christian's résumé.

It certainly did so for Mephibosheth. Talk about a redefined life. After assuming the throne of Saul, "David began wondering if anyone in Saul's family was still alive, for he had promised Jonathan that he would show kindness to them" (2 Sam. 9:1 NLT).

The Philistines, you'll remember, defeated Saul in battle. After the smoke of conflict passed, David sought to display mercy to Saul's descendants. A servant named Ziba remembered: "Yes, one of Jonathan's sons is still alive, but he is crippled" (v. 3 NLT). No name offered. Just the pain. Labeled by misfortune. An earlier chapter reveals the mishap. When word of Saul's and Jonathan's deaths reached the capital, a nurse in Jonathan's house swept up his five-year-old boy and fled. But in her haste, she stumbled and dropped him, crippling the boy in both feet.

Where does such a child turn? Can't walk. Can't work. Father and grandfather dead. Where can the crippled grandson of a failed leader go?

How about Lo-debar? Sounds like a place charm forgot. Like No Trees, Texas, or Weed, Oregon, or French Lick, Indiana. Lo-debar, Israel. Appropriate place for Mephibosheth. Stuck with a name longer than his arm. Dropped like a cantaloupe from a torn paper sack. How low can you go? Low enough to end up living in the low-rent district of Lo-debar.

Acquainted with its streets? If you've been dropped, you are. Dropped from the list. Dropped by a guy. Dropped by the team. Dropped off at the orphanage. And now you walk with a limp. People don't remember your name, but they remember your pain. "He's the alcoholic." "Oh, I remember her. The widow." "You mean the divorced woman from Nowheresville?" "No. Lo-debarville." You live labeled.

But then something Cinderella-like happens. The king's men knock on your Lo-debar door. They load you in a wagon and carry you into the presence of the king. You assume the worst and begin praying for a nonsnoring prison cellmate. But the servants don't deposit you on the jailhouse steps; they set you at the king's table. Right above your plate sits a place card bearing your name. "And from that time on, Mephibosheth ate regularly with David, as though he were one of his own sons" (v. 11 NLT).

Charles Swindoll has penned a galaxy of fine paragraphs. But my favorite is this imagined scene from David's palace.

Gold and bronze fixtures gleam from the walls. Lofty, wooden ceilings crown each spacious room. . . . David and his children gather for an evening meal. Absalom, tanned and handsome, is there, as is David's beautiful daughter Tamar. The call to dinner is given, and the king scans the room to see if all are present. One figure, though, is absent.

Clump, scraaape, clump, scraaape. The sound coming down the hall echoes into the chamber. *Clump, scraaape, clump, scraaape.* Finally, the person appears at the door and slowly shuffles to his seat. It is the lame Mephibosheth seated in grace at David's table. And the tablecloth covers his feet. Now the feast can begin.[1]

From Lo-debar to the palace, from obscurity to royalty, from no future to the king's table. Quite a move for Mephibosheth. Quite a reminder for us. He models our journey. God lifted us from the dead-end street of Lo-debarville and sat us at his table. "We are seated with him in the heavenly realms" (Eph. 2:6 NLT).

Marinate your soul in that verse. Next time the arid desert winds blow, defining you by yesterday's struggles, reach for God's goblet of grace and drink. Grace defines who you are. The parent you can't please is as mistaken as the doting uncle you can't disappoint. People hold no clout. Only God does. According to him, you are his. Period. "For we are God's masterpiece. He has created us anew in Christ Jesus, so that we can do the good things he planned for us long ago" (v. 10 NLT).

Suppose Mephibosheth had seen this verse. Imagine someone back in the Lo-debar days telling him, "Don't be discouraged, friend. I know you can't dance or run. Others kick the soccer ball, and you're stuck here staring out the window. But listen, God wrote your story. He cast you in his drama. Three thousand years from now your story will stir an image of grace for some readers in the twenty-first century."

Would he have believed it? I don't know. But I pray that you will. You hang as God's work of art, a testimony in his gallery of grace.

Over a hundred years ago, a group of fishermen were relaxing in the dining room of a Scottish seaside inn, trading fish stories. One of the men gestured widely, depicting the size of a fish that got away. His arm struck the serving maid's tea tray, sending the teapot flying into the whitewashed wall, where its contents left an irregular brown splotch.

The innkeeper surveyed the damage and sighed, "The whole wall will have to be repainted."

"Perhaps not," offered a stranger. "Let me work with it."

Having nothing to lose, the proprietor consented. The man pulled pencils, brushes, some jars of linseed oil, and pigment out of an art box. He sketched lines around the stains and dabbed shades and colors throughout the splashes of tea. In time, an image began to emerge: a stag with a great rack of antlers. The man inscribed his signature at the bottom, paid for his meal, and left. His name: Sir Edwin Landseer, famous painter of wildlife.

In his hands, a mistake became a masterpiece.[2]

God's hands do the same, over and over. He draws together the disjointed blotches in our life and renders them an expression of his love. We become pictures: "examples of the incredible wealth of his favor and kindness toward us" (v. 7 NLT).

Who determines your identity? What defines you? The day you were dropped? Or the day you were carried to the King's table?

Receive God's work. Drink deeply from his well of grace. As grace sinks deep into your soul, Lo-debar will become a dot in the rearview mirror. Dark days will define you no more. You're in the palace now.

And now you know what to say to the big brothers of this world. No need for frantic robe cleaning or rules for ring wearing. Your deeds don't save you. And your deeds don't keep you saved. Grace does. The next time big brother starts dispensing more snarls than twin Dobermans, loosen your sandals, set your ring on your finger, and quote the apostle of grace who said, "By the grace of God I am what I am" (1 Cor. 15:10 NKJV).

Questions for Reflection and Discussion

1. Describe the difference between "grace receiving" and "law keeping." Why does law keeping generally deflate joy? Read Galatians 1:6–7; 2:16. What most puzzled Paul about the choice his friends had made?

2. How do we sometimes try to earn our place at God's table?

3. How does God's grace of taking broken and hurting people and using their past pains, brokenness, and physical deformities bring glory to himself? In what way does grace shape how you live? How did it shape the way you acted today?

4. Read 2 Samuel 9:1–13. Why did David show such kindness to Mephibosheth (v. 1)? What would have been the result if Mephibosheth had tried to flee rather than go to the palace of the king? Are there times we flee from the King's presence and miss the blessing of sitting at his table?

5. How did Mephibosheth see himself (v. 8)? What privilege did Mephibosheth receive (v. 11)?

Chapter 20

JOSIAH

The people tore down the altars for the Baal gods as Josiah directed. Then Josiah cut down the incense altars that were above them. He broke up the Asherah idols and . . . beat them into powder. . . . He burned the bones of the priests on their own altars. . . . Josiah broke down the altars. . . . He cut down all the incense altars in all of Israel.

—2 Chronicles 34:4–5, 7

OVERCOMING YOUR HERITAGE

Stefan can tell you about family trees. He makes his living from them. He inherited a German forest that has been in his family for four hundred years. The trees he harvests were planted 180 years ago by his great-grandfather. The trees he plants won't be ready for market until his great-grandchildren are born.

He's part of a chain.

"Every generation must make a choice," he told me. "They can either pillage or plant. They can rape the landscape and get rich, or they can care for the landscape, harvest only what is theirs, and leave an investment for their children."[1]

Stefan harvests seeds sown by men he never knew.

Stefan sows seeds to be harvested by descendants he'll never see.

Dependent upon the past, responsible for the future: he's part of a chain.

Like us. Children of the past are we. Parents of the future. Heirs. Benefactors. Recipients of the work done by those before. Born into a forest we didn't seed.

Which leads me to ask, how's your forest?

As you stand on the land bequeathed by your ancestors, how does it look? How do you feel?

Pride at legacy left? Perhaps. Some inherit nourished soil. Deeply rooted trees of conviction. Row after row of truth and heritage. Could be that you stand in the forest of your fathers with pride. If so, give thanks, for many don't.

Many aren't proud of their family trees. Poverty. Shame. Abuse.

Such are the forests found by some of you. The land was pillaged. Harvest was taken, but no seed was sown.

Perhaps you were reared in a home of bigotry and so you are intolerant of minorities. Perhaps you were reared in a home of greed, hence your desires for possessions are insatiable.

Perhaps your childhood memories bring more hurt than inspiration. The voices of your past cursed you, belittled you, ignored you. At the time, you thought such treatment was typical. Now you see it isn't.

And now you find yourself trying to explain your past.

I came across a story of a man who must have had such thoughts. His heritage was tragic. His grandfather was a murderer and a mystic who sacrificed his own children in ritual abuse. His dad was a punk who ravaged houses of worship and made a mockery of believers. He was killed at the age of twenty-four . . . by his friends.

The men were typical of their era. They lived in a time when prostitutes purveyed their wares in houses of worship. Wizards treated disease with chants. People worshiped stars and followed horoscopes. More thought went into superstition and voodoo than into the education of the children.

It was a dark time in which to be born. What do you do when your grandfather followed black magic, your father was a scoundrel, and your nation is corrupt?

Follow suit? Some assumed he would. Branded him as a delinquent before he was born, a chip off the old rotten block. You can almost hear the people moan as he passes, "Gonna be just like his dad."

But they were wrong. He wasn't. He reversed the trend. He defied the odds. He stood like a dam against the trends of his day and rerouted the future of his nation. His achievements were so remarkable, we still tell his story twenty-six hundred years later.

The story of King Josiah. The world has seen wiser kings; the world has seen wealthier kings; the world has seen more powerful kings. But history has never seen a more courageous king than young Josiah.

Born some six hundred years before Jesus, Josiah inherited a fragile throne and a tarnished crown. The temple was in disarray, the Law was lost, and the people worshiped whatever god they desired. But by the end of Josiah's thirty-one-year reign, the temple had been rebuilt, the idols destroyed, and the law of God was once again elevated to a place of prominence and power.

The forest had been reclaimed.

Josiah's grandfather, King Manasseh, was remembered as the king who filled "Jerusalem from one end to the other with [the people's] blood" (2 Kings 21:16). His father, King Amon, died at the hands of his own officers. "He did what God said was wrong," reads his epitaph.

The citizens formed a posse and killed the assassins, and eight-year-old Josiah ascended the throne. Early in his reign Josiah made a brave choice. "He lived as his ancestor David had lived, and he did not stop doing what was right" (2 Kings 22:2).

He flipped through his family scrapbook until he found an ancestor worthy of emulation. Josiah skipped his dad's life and bypassed his grandpa's. He leapfrogged back in time until he found David and resolved, "I'm going to be like him."

The principle? We can't choose our parents, but we can choose our mentors.

And since Josiah chose David (who had chosen God), things began to happen.

> The people tore down the altars for the Baal gods as Josiah directed. Then Josiah cut down the incense altars that were above them. He broke up the Asherah idols and . . . beat them into powder. . . . He burned the bones of their priests on their own altars. . . . Josiah broke down the altars. . . . He cut down all the incense altars in all of Israel. (2 Chron. 34:4–5, 7)

Not what you call a public relations tour. But, then again, Josiah was not out to make friends. He was out to make a statement: "What my fathers taught, I don't teach. What they embraced, I reject."

And he wasn't finished. Four years later, at the age of twenty-six, he turned his attention to the temple. It was in shambles. The people had allowed it to fall into disrepair. But Josiah was determined. Something had happened that fueled his passion to restore the temple. A baton had been passed. A torch had been received.

Early in his reign he'd resolved to serve the God of his ancestor David. Now he chose to serve the God of someone else. Note 2 Chronicles 34:8: "In Josiah's eighteenth year as king, he made Judah and the Temple pure again. He sent Shaphan . . . to repair the Temple of the LORD, *the God of Josiah*" (emphasis added).

God was *his* God. David's faith was Josiah's faith. He had found the God of David and made him his own. As the temple was being rebuilt, one of the workers happened upon a scroll. On the scroll were the words of God given to Moses nearly a thousand years earlier.

When Josiah heard the words, he was shocked. He wept that his people had drifted so far from God that his Word was not a part of their lives.

He sent word to a prophetess and asked her, "What will become of our people?"

She told Josiah that since he had repented when he heard the words, his nation would be spared the anger of God (2 Chron. 34:27). Incredible. An entire generation received grace because of the integrity of one man.

Could it be that God placed him on earth for that reason?

Could it be that God has placed you on earth for the same?

Maybe your past isn't much to brag about. Maybe you've seen raw evil. And now you, like Josiah, have to make a choice. Do you rise above the past and make a difference? Or do you remain controlled by the past and make excuses?

Many choose the latter.

Many choose the convalescent homes of the heart. Healthy bodies. Sharp minds. But retired dreams. Back and forth they rock in the chair of regret, repeating the terms of surrender. Lean closely and you will hear them: "If only." The white flag of the heart.

"If only . . ."

"If only I'd been born somewhere else . . ."

"If only I'd been treated fairly . . ."

"If only I'd had kinder parents, more money, greater opportunities . . ."

"If only I'd been potty-trained sooner, spanked less, or taught to eat without slurping . . ."

Maybe you've used those words. Maybe you have every right to use them. Perhaps you, like Josiah, were hearing the ten count before you even got into the ring. For you to find an ancestor worth imitating, you, like Josiah, have to flip way back in your family album.

If such is the case, let me show you where to turn. Put down the scrapbook and pick up your Bible. Go to John's gospel and read Jesus' words: "Human life comes from human parents, but spiritual life comes from the Spirit" (John 3:6).

Think about that. Spiritual life comes from the Spirit! Your parents may have given you genes, but God gives you grace. Your parents may be responsible for your body, but God has taken charge of your soul. You may get your looks from your mother, but you get eternity from your Father, your heavenly Father.

By the way, he's not blind to your problems. In fact, God is willing to give you what your family didn't.

Didn't have a good father? He'll be your Father.

You are a son. And, if you are a son, then you are certainly an heir. (Gal. 4:7 PHILLIPS)

Didn't have a good role model? Try God.

You are God's children whom he loves, so try to be like him. (Eph. 5:1)

Never had a parent who wiped away your tears? Think again. God has noted each one.

You have seen me tossing and turning through the night. You have collected all my tears and preserved them in your bottle! You have recorded every one in your book. (Ps. 56:8 TLB)

God has not left you adrift on a sea of heredity. Just like Josiah, you cannot control the way your forefathers responded to God. But you can control the way you respond to him. The past does not have to be your prison. You have a voice in your destiny. You have a say in your life. You have a choice in the path you take.

Choose well and someday—generations from now—your grandchildren and great-grandchildren will thank God for the seeds you sowed.

Questions for Reflection and Discussion

1. "We can't choose our parents, but we can choose our mentors." What mentors have you chosen? Why did you choose the particular individuals?

2. Choose one word to describe how you feel about your past: Grateful? Angry? Discouraged? Proud? Depressed? Blessed?

3. How do we sometimes allow ourselves to be controlled by the past? Have you ever slipped into this mode? Explain.

4. "Spiritual life comes from the Spirit! Your parents may have given you genes, but God gives you grace." How does this principle change your outlook on your family history?

5. What sort of spiritual heritage do you have now? Describe it.

Chapter 21

◈

JOB

I had heard about you before, but now I have seen you.

—JOB 42:5 TLB

HE SPEAKS THROUGH
THE STORM

It all happened in one day. One day he could choose his tee time at the nicest golf course in the country; the next he couldn't even be the caddie. One day he could Learjet across the country to see the heavyweight bout at the Las Vegas Mirage. The next he couldn't afford a city bus across town.

Talk about calm becoming chaos . . .

The first thing to go is his empire. The market crashes; his assets tumble. What is liquid goes dry. What has been up goes down. Stocks go flat, and Job goes broke. There he sits in his leather chair at his soon-to-be-auctioned-off mahogany desk when the phone rings with news of calamity number two:

The kids were at a resort for the holidays when a storm blew in and took them with it.

Shell-shocked and dumbfounded, Job looks out the window into the sky that seems to be getting darker by the minute. He starts praying, telling God that things can't get any worse . . . and that's exactly what happens. He feels a pain in his chest that is more than last night's ravioli. The next thing he knows, he is bouncing in an ambulance with wires stuck to his chest and needles stuck in his arm.

He ends up tethered to a heart monitor in a community hospital room. Next to him lies an illegal immigrant who can't speak English.

Not, however, that Job lacks for conversation.

First there is his wife. Who could blame her for being upset at the week's calamities? Who could blame her for telling Job to curse God? But to curse God *and die*? If Job doesn't already feel abandoned, you know he does the minute his wife tells him to pull the plug and be done with it.

Then there are his friends. They have the bedside manner of a drill sergeant and the compassion of a chain-saw killer. A revised version of their theology might read like this: "Boy, you must have done something really bad! We know that God is good, so if bad things are happening to you, then you have been bad. Period."

Does Job take that lying down? Not hardly.

"You are doctors who don't know what they are doing," he says. "Oh, please be quiet! That would be your highest wisdom" (Job 13:4–5 TLB).

Translation? "Why don't you take your philosophy back to the pigpen where you learned it."

"I'm not a bad man," Job argues. "I paid my taxes. I'm active in civic duties. I'm a major contributor to United Way and a volunteer at the hospital bazaar."

Job is, in his eyes, a good man. And a good man, he reasons, deserves a good answer.

"Your suffering is for your own good," states Elihu, a young minister fresh out of seminary who hasn't lived long enough to be cynical and hasn't hurt enough to be quiet. He paces back and forth in the hospital room, with his Bible under his arm and his finger punching the air.

"God does all these things to a man—twice, even three times—to turn back his soul from the pit, that the light of life may shine on him" (Job 33:29–30 NIV).

Job follows his pacing like you'd follow a tennis player, head turning from side to side. What the young man says isn't bad theology, but it isn't much comfort either. Job steadily tunes him out and slides lower and lower under the covers. His head hurts. His eyes burn. His legs ache. And he can't stomach any more hollow homilies.

Yet his question still hasn't been answered:

"God, why is this happening to me?"

So God speaks.

Out of the thunder, he speaks. Out of the sky, he speaks. For all of us who would put ditto marks under Job's question and sign our names to it, he speaks.

- For the father who holds a rose taken off his son's coffin, he speaks.
- For the wife who holds the flag taken off her husband's casket, he speaks.
- For the couple with the barren womb and the fervent prayers, he speaks.
- For any person who has tried to see God through shattered glass, he speaks.
- For those of us who have dared to say, "If God is God, then . . ." God speaks.

He speaks out of the storm and into the storm, for that is where Job is. That is where God is best heard.

God's voice thunders in the room. Elihu sits down. Job sits up. And the two will never be the same again.

"Who is this that darkens my counsel with words without knowledge?" (Job 38:2 NIV).

Job doesn't respond.

"Brace yourself like a man; I will question you, and you shall answer me" (v. 3 NIV).

"Where were you when I laid the foundations of the earth? Tell me, if you know so much" (v. 4 TLB).

One question would have been enough for Job, but it isn't enough for God.

"Do you know how its dimensions were determined, and who did the surveying?" God asks. "What supports its foundations, and who laid its cornerstone, as the morning stars sang together and all the angels shouted for joy?" (vv. 5–7 TLB).

Questions rush forth. They pour like sheets of rain out of the clouds.

They splatter in the chambers of Job's heart with a wildness and a beauty and a terror that leave every Job who has ever lived drenched and speechless, watching the Master redefine who is who in the universe.

"Have you ever once commanded the morning to appear, and caused the dawn to rise in the east? Have you ever told the daylight to spread to the ends of the earth, to end the night's wickedness?" (vv. 12–13 TLB).

God's questions aren't intended to teach; they are intended to stun. They aren't intended to enlighten; they are intended to awaken. They aren't intended to stir the mind; they are intended to bend the knees.

"Has the location of the gates of Death been revealed to you? Do you realize the extent of the earth? Tell me about it if you know! Where does the light come from, and how do you get there? Or tell me about the darkness. Where does it come from? Can you find its boundaries, or go to its source? But of course you know all this! For you were born before it was all created, and you are so very experienced!" (vv. 17–21 TLB).

Finally Job's feeble hand lifts, and God stops long enough for him to respond. "I am nothing—how could I ever find the answers? I lay my hand upon my mouth in silence. I have said too much already" (Job 40:4–5 TLB).

God's message has connected:

- Job is a peasant, telling the King how to run the kingdom.
- Job is an illiterate, telling e. e. cummings to capitalize his personal pronouns.
- Job is the batboy, telling Babe Ruth to change his batting stance.
- Job is the clay, telling the potter not to press so hard.

"I owe no one anything," God declares in the crescendo of the wind. "Everything under the heaven is mine" (Job 41:11 TLB).

Job couldn't argue. God owes no one anything. No explanations. No excuses. No help. God has no debt, no outstanding balance, no favors to return. God owes no man anything.

Which makes the fact that he gave us everything even more astounding.

How you interpret this holy presentation is key. You can interpret God's hammering speech as a divine in-your-face tirade if you want. You can use the list of unanswerable questions to prove that God is harsh, cruel, and distant. You can use the book of Job as evidence that God gives us questions and no answers. But to do so, you need some scissors. To do so, you need to cut out the rest of the book of Job.

For that is not how Job heard it. All his life, Job had been a good man. All his life, he had believed in God. All his life, he had discussed God, had notions about him, and had prayed to him.

But in the storm Job sees him!

He sees Hope. Lover. Destroyer. Giver. Taker. Dreamer. Deliverer.

Job sees the tender anger of a God whose unending love is often received with peculiar mistrust. Job stands as a blade of grass against the consuming fire of God's splendor. Job's demands melt like wax as God pulls back the curtain and heaven's light falls uneclipsed across the earth.

Job sees God.

God could turn away at this point. The gavel has been slammed; the verdict has been rendered. The Eternal Judge has spoken.

Ah, but God is not angry with Job. Firm? Yes. Direct? No doubt. Clear and convincing? Absolutely. But angry? No.

God is never irritated by the candle of an honest seeker.

If you underline any passage in the book of Job, underline this one: "I had heard about you before, but now I have seen you" (Job 42:5 TLB).

Job sees God—and that is enough.

But it isn't enough for God.

The years to come find Job once again sitting behind his mahogany desk with health restored and profits up. His lap is once again full of children and grandchildren and great-grandchildren—for four generations!

If Job ever wonders why God doesn't bring back the children he had taken away, he doesn't ask. Maybe he doesn't ask because he knows that his children could never be happier than they are in the presence of this one he has seen so briefly.

Something tells me that Job would do it all again, if that's what it took to hear God's voice and stand in the Presence. Even if God left him with his bedsores and bills, Job would do it again.

For God gave Job more than Job ever dreamed. God gave Job Himself.

Questions for Reflection and Discussion

1. Describe the most difficult circumstance you've ever faced. Who was involved? What happened? How long did it last? Did you question or lash out at God during that time? What was the result? What did you learn through that experience?

2. Think about friends who "advised" you during a difficult time. What type of wisdom did they give you? What kind of advice have you given to others who have faced difficult times?

3. Read Job 1:8–12; 2:3–7. Why did God allow Job's difficult circumstances to occur? How does that knowledge add perspective to what happened to Job? Does that knowledge shed any light on the suffering in your life or in the life of someone you know? If so, explain.

4. Max writes that God is best heard in the storm. Do you agree? Why or why not?

5. When God finished speaking, Job said, "I had heard about you before, but now I have seen you" (Job 42:5 TLB). What did Job gain as a result of seeing God?

Chapter 22

❧

PETER

You prepare a table before me in the presence of my enemies.

—PSALM 23:5 NKJV

The Crowing
Rooster and Me

See the fellow in the shadows? That's Peter. Peter the apostle. Peter the impetuous. Peter the passionate. He once walked on water. Stepped right out of the boat onto the lake. He'll soon preach to thousands. Fearless before friends and foes alike. But tonight the one who stepped on the water has hurried into hiding. The one who will speak with power is weeping in pain.

Not sniffling or whimpering, but weeping. Bawling. Bearded face buried in thick hands. His howl echoing in the Jerusalem night. What hurts more? The fact that he did it? Or the fact that he swore he never would?

"Lord, I am ready to go with you to prison and even to die with you!" he pledged only hours earlier. "But Jesus said, 'Peter, before the rooster crows this day, you will say three times that you don't know me'" (Luke 22:33–34).

Denying Christ on the night of his betrayal was bad enough, but did he have to boast that he wouldn't? And one denial was pitiful, but three? Three denials were horrific, but did he have to curse? "Peter began to place a curse on himself and swear, 'I don't know the man'" (Matt. 26:74).

And now, awash in a whirlpool of sorrow, Peter is hiding. Peter is weeping. And soon Peter will be fishing.

We wonder why he goes fishing. We know why he goes to Galilee. He had been told that the risen Christ would meet the disciples there. The arranged meeting place is not the sea, however, but a mountain (Matt. 28:16). If the followers were to meet Jesus on a mountain, what are they doing in a boat? No one told them to fish, but that's what they did. "Simon Peter said, 'I am going out to fish.' The others said, 'We will go with you'" (John 21:3). Besides, didn't Peter quit fishing? Two years earlier, when Jesus called him to fish for men, didn't he drop his net and follow? We haven't seen him fish since. We never see him fish again. Why is he fishing now? Especially now! Jesus has risen from the dead. Peter has seen the empty tomb. Who could fish at a time like this?

Were they hungry? Perhaps that's the sum of it. Maybe the expedition was born out of growling stomachs.

Or then again, maybe it was born out of a broken heart.

You see, Peter could not deny his denial. The empty tomb did not erase the crowing rooster. Christ had returned, but Peter wondered, he must have wondered, "After what I did, would he return for someone like me?"

We've wondered the same. Is Peter the only person to do the very thing he swore he'd never do?

"Infidelity is behind me!"

"From now on, I'm going to bridle my tongue."

"No more shady deals. I've learned my lesson."

Oh, the volume of our boasting. And, oh, the heartbreak of our shame.

Rather than resist the flirting, we return it.

Rather than ignore the gossip, we share it.

Rather than stick to the truth, we shade it.

And the rooster crows, and conviction pierces, and Peter has a partner in the shadows. We weep as Peter wept, and we do what Peter did. We go fishing. We go back to our old lives. We return to our pre-Jesus practices. We do what comes naturally, rather than what comes spiritually. And we question whether Jesus has a place for folks like us.

Jesus answers that question. He answers it for you and me and all who tend to "Peter out" on Christ. His answer came on the shore of the sea in a gift to Peter. You know what Jesus did? Split the waters? Turn the boat to gold and the nets to silver? No, Jesus did something much more meaningful. He invited Peter to breakfast. Jesus prepared a meal.

Of course, the breakfast was one special moment among several that morning. There was the great catch of fish and the recognition of Jesus. The plunge of Peter and the paddling of the disciples. And there was the moment they reached the shore and found Jesus next to a fire of coals. The fish were sizzling, and the bread was waiting, and the defeater of hell and the ruler of heaven invited his friends to sit down and have a bite to eat.

No one could have been more grateful than Peter. The one Satan had sifted like wheat was eating bread at the hand of God. Peter was welcomed to the meal of Christ. Right there for the devil and his tempters to see, Jesus "prepared a table in the presence of his enemies."

Okay, so maybe Peter didn't say it that way. But David did. "You prepare a table before me in the presence of my enemies" (Ps. 23:5 NKJV). What the shepherd did for the sheep sounds a lot like what Jesus did for Peter.

At this point in the psalm, David's mind seems to be lingering in the high country with the sheep. Having guided the flock through the valley to the alp lands for greener grass, he remembers the shepherd's added responsibility. He must prepare the pasture.

This is new land, so the shepherd must be careful. Ideally, the grazing area will be flat, a mesa or tableland. The shepherd searches for poisonous plants and ample water. He looks for signs of wolves, coyotes, and bears.

Of special concern to the shepherd is the adder, a small brown snake that lives underground. Adders are known to pop out of their holes and nip the sheep on the nose. The bite often infects and can even kill. As defense against the snake, the shepherd pours a circle of oil at the top of each adder's hole. He also applies the oil to the noses of the animals. The oil on the snake's hole lubricates the exit, preventing the snake from climbing out. The smell of the oil on the sheep's nose drives the serpent away. The shepherd, in a very real sense, has prepared the table.[1]

What if your Shepherd did for you what the shepherd did for his flock? Suppose he dealt with your enemy, the devil, and prepared for you a safe place of nourishment? What if Jesus did for you what he did for Peter? Suppose he, in the hour of your failure, invited you to a meal?

What would you say if I told you he has done exactly that?

On the night before his death, Jesus prepared a table for his followers.

On the first day of the Festival of Unleavened Bread, the day the lambs for the Passover meal were killed, Jesus' disciples asked him, "Where do you want us to go and get the Passover meal ready for you?"

Then Jesus sent two of them with these instructions: "Go into the city, and a man carrying a jar of water will meet you. Follow him to the house he enters, and say to the owner of the house: 'The Teacher says, Where is the room where my disciples and I will eat the Passover meal?' Then he will show you a large upstairs room, fixed up and furnished, where you will get everything ready for us." (Mark 14:12–15 GNT)

Look who did the "preparing" here. Jesus reserved a large room and arranged for the guide to lead the disciples. Jesus made certain the room was furnished and the food set out. What did the disciples do? They faithfully complied and were fed.

The Shepherd prepared the table.

Not only that, he dealt with the snakes. You'll remember that only one of the disciples didn't complete the meal that night. "The devil had already persuaded Judas Iscariot, the son of Simon, to turn against Jesus" (John 13:2). Judas started to eat, but Jesus didn't let him finish. On the command of Jesus, Judas left the room. "'The thing that you will do—do it quickly.' . . . Judas took the bread Jesus gave him and immediately went out. It was night" (vv. 27, 30).

There is something dynamic in this dismissal. Jesus prepared a table in the presence of the enemy. Judas was allowed to see the supper, but he wasn't allowed to stay there.

You are not welcome here. This table is for my children. You may tempt them. You may trip them. But you will never sit with them. This is how much he loves us.

And if any doubt remains, lest there be any "Peters" who wonder if there is a place at the table for them, Jesus issues a tender reminder as he passes the cup. "Every one of you drink this. This is my blood which is the new agreement that God makes with his people. This blood is poured out for many to forgive their sins" (Matt. 26:27–28).

"*Every one* of you drink this." Those who feel unworthy, drink this. Those who feel ashamed, drink this. Those who feel embarrassed, drink this.

May I share a time when I felt all three?

By the age of eighteen I was well on my way to a drinking problem. My system had become so resistant to alcohol that a six-pack of beer had little or no impact on me. At the age of twenty, God not only saved me from hell after this life, he saved me from hell during it. Only he knows where I was headed, but I have a pretty good idea.

For that reason, part of my decision to follow Christ included no more beer. So I quit. But, curiously, the thirst for beer never left. It hasn't hounded me or consumed me, but two or three times a week the thought of a good beer sure entices me. Proof to me that I have to be careful is this—nonalcoholic beers have no appeal. It's not the flavor of the drink; it's the buzz. But for more than twenty years, drinking has never been a major issue.

A couple of years ago, however, it nearly became one. I lowered my guard a bit. *One beer with barbecue won't hurt.* Then another time with Mexican food. Then a time or two with no food at all. Over a period of two months I went from no beers to maybe one or two a week. Again, for most people, no problem, but for me it could become one.

You know when I began to smell trouble? One hot Friday afternoon I was on my way to speak at our annual men's retreat. Did I say the day was hot? Brutally hot. I was thirsty. Soda wouldn't do. So I began to plot. Where could I buy a beer and not be seen by anyone I knew?

With that thought, I crossed a line. What's done in secret is best not done at all. But I did it anyway. I drove to an out-of-the-way convenience store, parked, and waited until all patrons had left. I entered, bought my beer, held it close to my side, and hurried to the car.

That's when the rooster crowed.

It crowed because I was sneaking around. It crowed because I knew better. It crowed because, and this really hurt, the night before I'd scolded one of my daughters for keeping secrets from me. And now, what was I doing?

I threw the beer in the trash and asked God to forgive me. A few days later I shared my struggle with the elders and some members of the congregation and was happy to chalk up the matter to experience and move on.

But I couldn't. The shame plagued me. Of all the people to do such a thing. So many could be hurt by my stupidity. And of all the times to do such a thing. En route to minister at a retreat. What hypocrisy!

I felt like a bum. Forgiveness found its way into my head, but the elevator designed to lower it eighteen inches to my heart was out of order.

And, to make matters worse, Sunday rolled around. I found myself on the front row of the church, awaiting my turn to speak. Again, I had been honest with God, honest with the elders, honest with myself. But still, I struggled. Would God want a guy like me to preach?

The answer came in the Supper. The Lord's Supper. The same Jesus who'd prepared a meal for Peter had prepared one for me. The same Shepherd who had trumped the devil trumped him again. The same Savior who had built a fire on the shore stirred a few embers in my heart.

"Every one of you drink this." And so I did. It felt good to be back at the table.

QUESTIONS FOR REFLECTION AND DISCUSSION

1. Describe a time when you followed Peter's example and did the very thing you swore you'd never do. What happened?

2. Have you ever "gone fishing" or returned to your pre-Jesus practices after a spiritual failure? If so, how did you feel at that time?

3. Why do we question whether Jesus has a place for people like us? Have you ever felt that way? Explain.

4. Why do you think Jesus allowed Judas to see the Lord's Supper? Why not banish him before the disciples gathered?

5. How do the stories of both Peter and Max show true repentance? How does Jesus always respond to true repentance? Why is this important to understand?

Chapter 23

THE THIEF ON THE CROSS

One of the criminals who hung there hurled insults at him: "Aren't you the Christ? Save yourself and us!"

But the other criminal rebuked him. "Don't you fear God," he said, "since you are under the same sentence? We are punished justly, for we are getting what our deeds deserve. But this man has done nothing wrong."

Then he said, "Jesus, remember me when you come into your kingdom."

Jesus answered him, "I tell you the truth, today you will be with me in paradise."

—LUKE 23:39–43 NIV

THE TALE OF THE
CRUCIFIED CROOK

The only thing more outlandish than the request was that it was granted. Just trying to picture the scene is enough to short-circuit the most fanciful of imaginations; a flatnosed ex-con asking God's Son for eternal life? But trying to imagine the appeal being honored, well, that steps beyond the realm of reality and enters absurdity.

But as absurd as it may appear, that's exactly what happened. He who deserved hell got heaven, and we are left with a puzzling riddle. What, for goodness' sake, was Jesus trying to teach us? What was he trying to prove by pardoning this strong-arm, who in all probability had never said grace, much less done anything to deserve it?

Well, I've got a theory. But to explain it, I've got to tell you a tale that you may not believe.

It seems a couple of prowlers broke into a department store in a large city. They successfully entered the store, stayed long enough to do what they came to do, and escaped unnoticed. What is unusual about the story is what these fellows did. They took nothing. Absolutely nothing. No merchandise was stolen. No items were removed. But what they did do was ridiculous.

Instead of stealing anything, they changed the cost of everything. Price tags were swapped. Values were exchanged. These clever pranksters took the tag off a $395.00 camera and stuck it on a $5.00 box of stationery. The $5.95 sticker on a paperback book was removed and placed on an outboard motor. They repriced everything in the store!

Crazy? You bet. But the craziest part of this story took place the next morning. (You are not going to believe this.) The store opened as usual. Employees went to work. Customers began to shop. The place functioned as normal for four hours before anyone noticed what had happened.

Four hours! Some people got some great bargains. Others got fleeced. For four solid hours no one noticed that all the values had been swapped.

Hard to believe? It shouldn't be—we see the same thing happening every day. We are deluged by a distorted value system. We see the most valuable things in our lives peddled for pennies and we see the cheapest smut go for millions.

The examples are abundant and besetting. Here are a few that I've encountered in the last week.

The salesman who defended his illegal practices by saying, "Let's not confuse business with ethics."

The military men who sold top-secret information (as well as their integrity) for $6,000.

The cabinet member of a large nation who was caught illegally dealing in semiprecious stones. His cabinet position? Minister of *Justice*.

The father who confessed to the murder of his twelve-year-old daughter. The reason he killed her? She refused to go to bed with him.

Why do we do what we do? Why do we take blatantly black-and-white and paint it gray? Why are priceless mores trashed while senseless standards are obeyed? What causes us to elevate the body and degrade the soul? What causes us to pamper the skin while we pollute the heart?

Our values are messed up. Someone broke into the store and exchanged all the price tags. Thrills are going for top dollar and the value of human beings is at an all-time low.

One doesn't have to be a philosopher to determine what caused such a sag in the market. It all began when someone convinced us that the human race is headed nowhere. That man has no *destiny*. That we are in a cycle. That there is no reason or rhyme to this absurd existence. Somewhere we got the idea that we are meaninglessly trapped on a puny mud heap that has no destination. The earth is just a spinning mausoleum and the universe is purposeless. The creation was incidental and humanity has no direction.

Pretty gloomy, huh?

The second verse is even worse. If man has no destiny, then he has no *duty*. No obligation, no responsibility. If man has no destiny, then he has no guidelines or goals. If man has no destiny, then who is to say what is right or wrong? Who is to say that a husband can't leave his wife and family? Who is to say you can't abort a fetus? What is wrong with shacking up? Who says I can't step on someone's neck to get to the top? It's your value system against mine. No absolutes. No principles. No ethics. No standards. Life is reduced to weekends, paychecks, and quick thrills. The bottom line is disaster.

"The existentialist," wrote existentialist Jean-Paul Sartre, "finds it extremely embarrassing that God does not exist, for there disappears with him all possibility of finding values in an intelligible heaven. . . . Everything is indeed permitted if God does not exist, and man is in consequence forlorn, for he cannot find anything to depend on within or without himself."[1]

If man has no duty or destiny, the next logical step is that man has no *value*. If man has no future, he isn't worth much. He is worth, in fact, about as much as a tree or a rock. No difference. There is no reason to be here; therefore, there is no value.

And you've seen the results of this. Our system goes haywire. We feel useless and worthless. We freak out. We play games. We create false value systems. We say that you are valuable if you are pretty. We say that you are valuable if you can produce. We say that you are valuable if you can slam-dunk a basketball or snag a pop fly. You are valuable if your name has a "Dr." in front of it or PhD on the end of it. You are valuable if you have a six-figure salary and drive a foreign car.

Value is now measured by two criteria: appearance and performance.

Pretty tough system, isn't it? Where does that leave the retarded? Or the ugly or uneducated? Where does that place the aged or the handicapped? What hope does that offer the unborn child? Not much. Not much at all. We become nameless numbers on mislaid lists.

Now please understand, this is man's value system. It is not God's. His plan is much brighter. God, with eyes twinkling, steps up to the philosopher's blackboard, erases the never-ending, ever-repeating circle of history, and replaces it with a line—a hope-filled, promising, slender line. And, looking over his shoulder to see if the class is watching, he draws an arrow on the end.

In God's book man is heading somewhere. He has an amazing destiny. We are being prepared to walk down the church aisle and become the bride of Jesus. We are going to live with him. Share the throne with him. Reign with him. We count. We are valuable. And what's more, our worth is built in! Our value is inborn.

You see, if there was anything that Jesus wanted everyone to understand it was this: a person is worth something simply because he is a person. That is why he treated people like he did. Think about it. The girl caught making undercover thunder with someone she shouldn't—he forgave her. The untouchable leper who asked for cleansing—he touched him. The blind welfare case that cluttered the roadside—he honored him. And the worn-out old windbag addicted to self-pity near the pool of Siloam—he healed him!

And don't forget the classic case study on the value of a person by Luke. It is called "The Tale of the Crucified Crook."

If anyone was ever worthless, this one was. If any man ever deserved dying, this man probably did. If any fellow was ever a loser, this fellow was at the top of the list.

Perhaps that is why Jesus chose him to show us what he thinks of the human race.

Maybe this criminal had heard the Messiah speak. Maybe he had seen him love the lowly. Maybe he had watched him dine with the punks, pickpockets, and pot mouths on the streets. Or maybe not. Maybe the only thing he knew about this Messiah was what he now saw: a beaten, slashed, nail-suspended preacher. His face crimson with blood, his bones peeking through torn flesh, his lungs gasping for air.

Something, though, told him he had never been in better company. And somehow he realized that even though all he had was prayer, he had finally met the one to whom he should pray.

"Any chance that you could put in a good word for me?" (Loose translation.)

"Consider it done."

Now why did Jesus do that? What in the world did he have to gain by promising this desperado a place of honor at the banquet table? What in the world could this chiseling quisling ever offer in return? I mean, the Samaritan woman I can understand. She could go back and tell the tale. And Zacchaeus had some money that he could give. But this guy? What is he going to do? Nothing!

That's the point. Listen closely. Jesus' love does not depend upon what we do for him. Not at all. In the eyes of the King, you have value simply because you are. You don't have to look nice or perform well. Your value is inborn.

Period.

Think about that for just a minute. You are valuable just because you exist. Not because of what you do or what you have done, but simply because you are. Remember that. Remember that the next time you are left bobbing in the wake of someone's steamboat ambition. Remember that the next time some trickster tries to hang a bargain basement price tag on your self-worth. The next time someone tries to pass you off as a cheap buy, just think about the way Jesus honors you . . . and smile.

I do. I smile because I know I don't deserve love like that. None of us do. When you get right down to it, any contribution that any of us makes is pretty puny. All of us—even the purest of us—deserve heaven about as much as that crook did. All of us are signing on Jesus' credit card, not ours.

And it also makes me smile to think that there is a grinning ex-con walking the golden streets who knows more about grace than a thousand theologians. No one else would have given him a prayer. But in the end that is all that he had. And in the end, that is all it took.

No wonder they call him the Savior.

QUESTIONS FOR REFLECTION AND DISCUSSION

1. What gives a person value, according to today's culture? What affects society's view of the worth of the individual?

2. What do the following passages teach about the value God places upon people: Romans 5:8; Ephesians 2:4–5; Titus 3:4–7; 1 John 4:9–10?

3. Do we behave as if we have intrinsic value? If people truly believed they had intrinsic value, what problems in society would no longer exist?

4. Read Luke 23:32–43. What can you learn about the two criminals from this brief episode? Why do you think Jesus gave this criminal a promise of paradise?

5. How do you think the crucified crook would explain grace in one sentence?

NOTES

CHAPTER 2: SIMON AND MARY

1. Matthew waits until chapter 26 to tell a story that chronologically should appear in chapter 20. By referring to John's gospel we see the anointing by Mary in Bethany occurred on Saturday night (John 12:1). Why does Matthew wait until so late to record the story? It appears that he sometimes elevates theme over chronology. The last week of Christ's life is a week of bad news. Chapters 26 and 27 sing the woeful chorus of betrayal. First the leaders, then Judas, then the apostles, Peter, Pilate, and eventually all the people turn against Jesus. Perhaps with the desire to tell one good story of faith in the midst of so many ones of betrayal, Matthew waits until Matthew 26 to tell of Simon and Mary.

CHAPTER 4: CORNELIUS

1. Gavan Daws, *Holy Man; Father Damien of Molokai* (Honolulu: University of Hawaii Press, 1984).
2. Alfred Edersheim, *The Life and Times of Jesus the Messiah*, unabridged edition (Peabody, MA: Hendrickson Publishers, 1993), 62–63.
3. Bob Ray Sanders, *"Blossom's in the Dust* Movie Fine, but the Woman Was Amazing,"* Fort Worth Star-Telegram*, November 17, 2002, www.angelfire.com /tx5/adoptee/sanders.html.

CHAPTER 8: NOAH

1. Charles Swindoll, *The Tale of the Tardy Oxcart and 1,501 Other Stories* (Nashville: Word Publishing, 1998), 275.

CHAPTER 10: PETER AND JOHN

1. CIA, *The World Factbook*, 2009, https://www.cia.gov/library/publications /the-world-factbook/geos/tu.html.
2. *Malatya: The Story of the First Martyrs of the Modern Turkish Church*, www .malatyafilm.com.
3. CIA, *The World Factbook*, 2009.
4. dc Talk and the Voice of the Martyrs, *Jesus Freaks: Stories of Those Who Stood for Jesus; The Ultimate Jesus Freaks* (Tulsa, OK: Albury Publishing, 1999), 208–9.

CHAPTER 12: ANANIAS AND SAUL
1. Not to be confused with the Ananias of Acts 5.

CHAPTER 13: DAVID
1. *San Antonio Express News*, "Does Texan have a prayer of trading domain name?" April 23, 2005.

CHAPTER 15: THE CRIPPLED MAN AT THE BEAUTIFUL GATE
1. UNICEF, *The State of the World's Children 2009: Maternal and Newborn Health*, www.unicef.org/sowc09/report/report.php.
2. James Strong, *New Strong's Exhaustive Concordance* (Nashville: Thomas Nelson, 1996), s.v. "compassion."
3. Bill Gates Sr. with Mary Ann Makin, *Showing Up for Life: Thoughts on the Gifts of a Lifetime* (New York: Broadway Books, 2009), 155.

CHAPTER 16: ISAIAH
1. Darren Brown, ed., *The Greatest Exploration Stories Ever Told: The Tales of Search and Discovery* (Guilford, CT: Lyons Press, 2003), 207–19.
2. Ibid., 223.
3. Jerry Bridges, *The Pursuit of Holiness* (Colorado Springs: NavPress, 1978), 64.
4. Edward W. Goodrick and John R. Kohlenberger, *Zondervan NIV Exhaustive Concordance*, 2nd ed., James A. Swanson, ed. (Grand Rapids: Zondervan, 1999), 1487.

CHAPTER 17: THE GADARENE DEMONIAC
1. Not her real name.
2. Linda Dillow and Lorraine Pintus, *Gift-Wrapped by God: Secret Answers to the Question, "Why Wait?"* (Colorado Springs, CO: WaterBrook Press, 2002), 59–64.

CHAPTER 18: THE LEPER JESUS HEALED
1. Not his actual name.

CHAPTER 19: MEPHIBOSHETH
1. Charles Swindoll, *The Tale of the Tardy Oxcart and 1,501 Other Stories* (Nashville: Word Publishing, 1998), 250.
2. Ron Lee Davis with James D. Denny, *Mistreated* (Portland, OR: Multnomah Press, 1989), 147–48.

CHAPTER 20: JOSIAH

1. With appreciation to Stefan Richart-Willmes.

CHAPTER 22: PETER

1. Charles W. Slemming, *He Leadeth Me: The Shepherd's Life in Palestine* (Fort Washington, PA: Christian Literature Crusade, 1964), quoted in Charles R. Swindoll, *Living Beyond the Daily Grind, Book 1: Reflections on the Songs and Sayings in Scripture* (Nashville: W Publishing Group, 1988), 77–78.

CHAPTER 23: THE THIEF ON THE CROSS

1. Walter Kaufman, ed., *Existentialism from Dostoyevsky to Sartre* (New York: Meridian Books, 1956), 294–95.

SOURCES

All of the material in *Cast of Characters: Lost & Found* was originally published in books authored by Max Lucado. All copyrights to the original works are held by Max Lucado.

Jairus: *He Still Moves Stones*, chapter 17.

Simon and Mary: *And the Angels Were Silent*, chapter 6.

Jacob: *God Came Near*, chapter 28.

Cornelius: *Outlive Your Life*, chapter 14.

Woman with the Issue of Blood, The: *He Still Moves Stones*, chapter 7.

Philip: *Outlive Your Life*, chapter 12.

The Paralyzed Man: *He Still Moves Stones*, chapter 12.

Noah: *A Love Worth Giving*, chapter 14.

Woman Caught in Adultery, The: *He Still Moves Stones*, chapter 2.

Peter and John: *Outlive Your Life*, chapter 8.

Nicodemus: *He Still Moves Stones*, chapter 13.

Ananias and Saul: *Outlive Your Life*, chapter 13.

David: *Facing Your Giants*, chapter 16

Jesus' Brothers: *He Still Moves Stones*, chapter 4.

Crippled Man at the Beautiful Gate, The: *Outlive Your Life*, chapter 7.

Isaiah: *It's Not About Me*, chapter 4.

Gadarene Demoniac, The: *Next Door Savior*, chapter 8.

Leper Jesus Healed, The: *Just Like Jesus*, chapter 3.

Mephibosheth: *Come Thirsty*, chapter 3.

Josiah: *When God Whispers Your Name*, chapter 15.

Job: *In the Eye of the Storm*, chapter 17.

Peter: *Traveling Light*, chapter 14.

Thief on the Cross, The: *No Wonder They Call Him the Savior*, chapter 4.

The Lucado Reader's Guide

Discover . . . Inside every book by Max Lucado, you'll find words of encouragement and inspiration that will draw you into a deeper experience with Jesus and treasures for your walk with God. What will you discover?

3:16: The Numbers of Hope
. . . the 26 words that can change your life.
core scripture: John 3:16

And the Angels Were Silent
. . . what Jesus Christ's final days can teach you about what matters most.
core scripture: Matthew 20–27

The Applause of Heaven
. . . the secret to a truly satisfying life.
core scripture: The Beatitudes, Matthew 5:1–10

Come Thirsty
. . . how to rehydrate your heart and sink into the wellspring of God's love.
core scripture: John 7:37–38

Cure for the Common Life
. . . the unique things God designed you to do with your life.
core scripture: 1 Corinthians 12:7

Facing Your Giants
. . . when God is for you, no challenge is too great.
core scripture: 1 and 2 Samuel

Fearless
. . . how faith is the antidote to the fear in your life.
core scripture: John 14:1,3

A Gentle Thunder
. . . the God who will do whatever it takes to lead his children back to Him.
core scripture: Psalm 81:7

Great Day Every Day
. . . how living in a purposeful way will help you trust more, stress less.
core scripture: Psalm 118:24

The Great House of God
. . . a blueprint for peace, joy, and love found in the Lord's Prayer.
core scripture: The Lord's Prayer, Matthew 6:9–13

God Came Near
. . . a love so great that it left heaven to become part of your world.
core scripture: John.1:14

He Chose the Nails
. . . a love so deep that it chose death on a cross—just to win your heart.
core scripture: 1 Peter 1:18–20

He Still Moves Stones
. . . the God who still does the impossible—in your life.
core scripture: Matthew 12:20

In the Eye of the Storm
. . . peace in the storms of your life.
core scripture: John 6

In the Grip of Grace
. . . the greatest gift of all—the grace of God.
core scripture: Romans

It's Not About Me
. . . why focusing on God will make sense of your life.
core scripture: 2 Corinthians 3:18

Just Like Jesus
. . . a life free from guilt, fear, and anxiety.
core scripture: Ephesians 4:23–24

A Love Worth Giving
. . . how living loved frees you to love others.
core scripture: 1 Corinthians 13

Next Door Savior
. . . a God who walked life's hardest trials—and still walks with you through yours.
core scripture: Matthew 16:13–16

No Wonder They Call Him the Savior
. . . hope in the unlikeliest place—upon the cross.
core scripture: Romans 5:15

Outlive Your Life
. . . that a great God created you to do great things.
core scripture: Acts 1

Six Hours One Friday
. . . forgiveness and healing in the middle of loss and failure.
core scripture: John 19–20

Traveling Light
. . . the power to release the burdens you were never meant to carry.
core scripture: Psalm 23

When God Whispers Your Name
. . . the path to hope in knowing that God knows you, never forgets you, and cares about the details of your life.
core scripture: John 10:3

When Christ Comes
. . . why the best is yet to come.
core scripture: 1 Corinthians 15:23

Recommended reading if you're struggling with . . .

FEAR AND WORRY
Come Thirsty
Fearless
For the Tough Times
Next Door Savior
Traveling Light

GRIEF/DEATH OF A LOVED ONE
Next Door Savior
Traveling Light
When Christ Comes
When God Whispers Your Name

GUILT
In the Grip of Grace
Just Like Jesus

LONELINESS
God Came Near

SIN
Facing Your Giants
He Chose the Nails
Six Hours One Friday

DISCOURAGEMENT
He Still Moves Stones
Next Door Savior

WEARINESS
When Got Whispers Your Name

Recommended reading if you want to know more about . . .

THE CROSS
And the Angels Were Silent
He Chose the Nails
No Wonder They Call Him the Savior
Six Hours One Friday

GRACE
He Chose the Nails
In the Grip of Grace

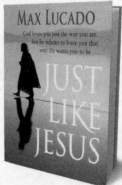

HEAVEN
The Applause of Heaven
When Christ Comes

SHARING THE GOSPEL
God Came Near
No Wonder They Call Him the Savior

Recommended reading if you're looking for more . . .

COMFORT

For the Tough Times
He Chose the Nails
Next Door Savior
Traveling Light

COMPASSION

Outlive Your Life

COURAGE

Facing Your Giants
Fearless

HOPE

3:16: The Numbers of Hope
Facing Your Giants
A Gentle Thunder
God Came Near

JOY

The Applause of Heaven
Cure for the Common Life
When God Whispers Your Name

LOVE

Come Thirsty
A Love Worth Giving
No Wonder They Call Him the Savior

PEACE

And the Angels Were Silent
The Great House of God
In the Eye of the Storm
Traveling Light

SATISFACTION

And the Angels Were Silent
Come Thirsty
Cure for the Common Life
Every Day Deserves a Chance

TRUST

A Gentle Thunder
It's Not About Me
Next Door Savior

Max Lucado books make great gifts!

If you're coming up to a special occasion, consider one of these.

FOR ADULTS:

For the Tough Times
Grace for the Moment
Live Loved
The Lucado Life Lessons Study Bible
Mocha with Max
DaySpring Daybrighteners® and cards

FOR TEENS/GRADUATES:

Let the Journey Begin
You Can Be Everything God Wants You to Be
You Were Made to Make a Difference

FOR KIDS:

Just in Case You Ever Wonder
The Oak Inside the Acorn
You Are Special

FOR PASTORS AND TEACHERS:

God Thinks You're Wonderful
You Changed My Life

AT CHRISTMAS:

The Crippled Lamb
Christmas Stories from Max Lucado
God Came Near